An Unsolicited Gift

DR DENNIS FRIEDMAN is a Fellow of the Royal College of Psychiatrists. He has published innovative work in the fields of anxiety management, stress-related illness and the treatment of phobias. He is the author of three successful psychological biographies: *Inheritance: A Psychological History of the Royal Family*; *Darling Georgie: The Enigma of King George V*; and *Ladies of the Bedchamber: The Role of the Royal Mistress*. He is married to author and playwright Rosemary Friedman and lives in London.

An Unsolicited Gift

Why We Do What We Do

Dennis Friedman

ARCADIA BOOKS

Arcadia Books Ltd
15–16 Nassau Street
London W1W 7AB

www.arcadiabooks.co.uk

First published by Arcadia Books 2010

A catalogue record for this book is available from the British Library.

ISBN 978-1-906413-60-6

Typeset in Minion by MacGuru Ltd
Printed and bound in Finland by WS Bookwell

Arcadia Books gratefully acknowledges the financial support of Arts Council England.

Arcadia Books supports English PEN, the fellowship of writers who work together to promote literature and its understanding. English PEN upholds writers' freedoms in Britain and around the world, challenging political and cultural limits on free expression. To find out more, visit www.englishpen.org or contact
English PEN, 6-8 Amwell Street, London EC1R 1UQ

Arcadia Books distributors are as follows:

in the UK and elsewhere in Europe:
Turnaround Publishers Services
Unit 3, Olympia Trading Estate
Coburg Road
London N22 6TZ

in the US and Canada:
Independent Publishers Group
814 N. Franklin Street
Chicago, IL 60610

in Australia:
Tower Books
PO Box 213
Brookvale, NSW 2100

in New Zealand:
Addenda
PO Box 78224
Grey Lynn
Auckland

in South Africa:
Jacana Media (Pty) Ltd
PO Box 291784,
Melville 2109
Johannesburg

Arcadia Books is the *Sunday Times* Small Publisher of the Year 2002/03

Contents

Thanks are due to: Shirley Conran, Peter Day, Peter James, Debbie Lennard, Dr Cathie O'Driscoll, Daniela de Groote, Dan Toller, Gary Pulsifer, Keith Richens, Professor Hugh Freeman, Angeline Rothermundt, and my wife, Rosemary Friedman, for her invaluable help with this book.

For Rosemary

'They fuck you up, your mum and dad.'

Philip Larkin

*'All happy families are alike but an unhappy family
is unhappy after its own fashion.'*

Leo Tolstoy

Foreword

More than a hundred years have passed since Sigmund Freud realised that the unconscious mind contained answers to questions that
most people had never considered asking. No one had previously
thought to explore the inner world the better to understand the
outer one. In a milieu dedicated to fast food, speed dating, sound
bites and the ten-minute NHS primary care consultation, there is
seldom time to consider the bio-psycho-social background to health
problems or the importance of the role played by mothering. The
fallout from this could result in an antisocial pandemic as damaging to communal health as is a flu pandemic to physical health. An
important contribution to the welfare of children, and by extension
to society, might well be made by taking sufficient time to consider
the vital interaction between a new mother and her child. This is not
a 'how-to book' or even a 'how-not to' book. It is an illustration of
the power of parenting.

Note: For he, read he/she.

Introduction

A mother gives life to her child. It is his birthday gift from her. An understanding of his needs is an essential component of the gift as is the loving concern shown him by his parents throughout his upbringing.

The mother's role – at least to begin with – is the more important. She is the child's introduction to a strange new world. Being 'abroad' for the first time takes getting used to. The child does not understand the language. There is no guidebook, no commonly used phrases to help him voice needs which had never previously existed for him. He feels cold. He feels hungry. He feels uncomfortable. He looks to his mother for comfort, to introduce him to his new environment, and to satisfy his needs. It is his entitlement. If she is unable to do this he will look to others to satisfy it later, sometimes in ways that are socially inappropriate.

His parents' initial response to him is (almost) always one of love and an overwhelming concern for his welfare. Decisions are made as to whether to satisfy his hunger when he cries, or to pick him up when he wakes. A sensitive mother will observe his body language and respond to it using babble talk. Less sensitive mothers may take longer to engage in this conversation. But what if the conversation never takes place? Will the child as an adult, expect someone else to understand him? Employing another woman – an au pair or a nanny – may be a necessary option in infancy, but in adulthood an involvement with another woman will merely reinforce what he was denied in childhood, the right to a unique, ongoing, caring commitment with one loving partner.

Parental love may be absent or abusive, disappointing, overwhelming or if it is conditional on the child being pleasing, an investment. If it is absent or disappointing, a vacuum of need will be created which the child will be drawn to fill throughout his life in a variety of ways. If love is abusive he will be hurt and angry and may later victimise others. If love is overwhelming he will find it difficult to break away from and may remain a child. Only if his relationship with his parents has provided him with contentment, will stable adult relationships be guaranteed. Can he alter his destiny? Can he make up his own mind as to where it lies? Bond-power may sometimes be stronger than will-power. But by understanding the nature of the bond the adult will be able to modify his lifestyle to one suited to his abilities and his talents.

We need to know about our upbringing and our reaction to it. It may not easily be recalled but reflections of it occur in every aspect of life. We need to know what has disposed us to crime rather than law enforcement, to a life on the streets rather than one in the caring professions; why we chose medicine over the media or golf over tennis. Why we are photographers rather than models, surgeons rather than psychiatrists, demolition workers rather than bricklayers, nurses rather than call girls. We need to know why we are drawn to paint rather than to write, become stock market dealers rather than car salesmen, prefer romance to reality, or choose to live in the world of the imagination rather than the real world. And why do we need to know? Because understanding what has influenced us to choose what we do and why we do it will help us make better use of our unsolicited gift.

Children with few inner resources will grow up to look outside themselves to source the missing component of their birthday gift. Sexual promiscuity, the misuse of chemicals, risk-taking and crime provide a quick fix. Those who solicit sex from women, or seek the illusion of security through financial fraud, who look for highs by risking their lives and the lives of others by living dangerously, are likely to be re-enacting a time when the two people they might have expected to provide them with love and security failed to do so.

There are ways other than criminal to relieve temporarily the shortcomings of early life. Explosive outbursts, envy, jealousy, sibling rivalry and love/hate relationships – often found in teenage gangs which provide their members with 'alternative families' – may provide useful safety valves. But violence is too often triggered and others scapegoated. While gang members act out antisocial atti-tudes, unwittingly encouraged perhaps by baffled or unavailable parents, other victims of disturbed upbringings may be able to talk out their problems with friends, or in therapy, or find fulfilment in creative activity.

Crime is the most damaging of all the many lifestyles for which parents may be responsible. If a child has not been provided with sufficient love there are other ways for him to acquire it than to steal it. It is never too late for children to 'think out' their reaction to their unsolicited gift in their own homes rather than 'act it out' in the homes of others. It is never too late for parents to avoid passing on to their children the more negative aspects of the gift. By recognising damaging patterns, their adult children will be provided with an opportunity to change the effects of them. Antisocial reactions to a deprived past may never be entirely eradicated. They can be modified when insight is acquired into nurturing skills by parents, and more creative reactions to them considered by children. Couples who live together, who do not abuse their children, who are not addicted to chemicals and have provided well chosen carers while they are not themselves available, may believe that they have done enough to ensure their child is free to choose a creative lifestyle rather than a destructive one. This is not always so. Autocracy may take over from democracy in the family unit as boundaries and guidelines become necessary. The reasons behind parental demands may be queried. The response 'because I say so', if used routinely, rather than as occasional short-hand, is unacceptable. At best it will suppress curiosity which one day might stand the adult in good stead. At worst it could lead to the deadening of a vital spark. The mother/child partnership, and later the father/child partnership, should ideally be as one between equals; a democratic unit where issues are debated using body language and mother tongue.

Parents cannot fail to be aware of the immediate effects they have on the behavioural responses of their child but they are less aware of the more remote effects on later life events. Some children may be penalised twice, once if their nurturing and feeding needs are inadequately met and again by being encouraged by parents into an unfulfilling lifestyle unsuited to their potential.

Some adults believe that they have found compensation for their unhappy childhoods when they fall in love. But the repetition of the 'primary love affair' with another 'mother' will often leave them as disappointed with their new partner as they were with their first one. Having sought gratification and an illusory compensation, from punishing others for the shortcomings of parents, and finding neither an appropriate outlet for anger nor any recompense for it, a few will turn their murderous rage upon themselves. Unable to cope with one loss too many, they may be tempted to discard their unsolicited gift together with the wrapping it came in.

Those who dispose of their lives do so because they are unaware that the wrapping in which the gift came is never entirely empty. No matter how unloving their parents, they will have provided their children not only with life but, at the very least, the potential to make good use of it. Those who understand this will acknowledge, possibly for the first time, that they do possess inner resources. Sparks of appreciation feed upon themselves and are life-enhancing; sparks of resentment feed upon themselves and are death-enhancing. Some will gamble with their most valuable possession. With nothing to lose and everything to gain, their priceless gift may be destroyed. Not all high-risk involvements (death in the face of the enemy, death in the face of adversity) carry the stigma of self-harm, but believing that fate has made the decision, those who gamble with their lives consider that they cannot be held responsible for the outcome.

Risk-taking, often confused with bravery, reveals an indifference to life in those who lack the courage to end it. To lay down one's life for others may be posthumously rewarded: to lay down one's life for oneself is considered cowardly by those who have never experienced loss. Gamblers who play with money expect to win but seldom do, gamblers who play with their lives expect to lose and often do. A high level of arousal, which may temporarily relieve loss-induced depression, is the upside of 'dicing with death'. The downside is death.

Deconstructing creativity as well as deconstructing destructiveness provides insight into the power and influence of parents. It will help them to recognise the importance of providing their children with sufficient love and information to reduce the risk of their growing up to endanger the lives of others by, at worst, turning to crime, or at best adopting a lifestyle inappropriate to their potential.

Those, equally emotionally deprived, but whose genetic endowment has provided them with talent and a sense of purpose, may find outlets for their frustrated needs through creativity. The positive feedback provided by appreciation of their writing, painting, composition or performance may compensate for some of the psychological deficits of their early infancy.

Parents, who in many cases have perpetuated the mistakes made earlier by their own parents or at best have reversed them, are as responsible for the social conduct of their children as is their biological make-up and their genetic inheritance. 'How-to' books may help them care 'for' a child, but in order to care 'about' a child, they need to understand how their own upbringing has influenced their parenting attitudes.

Uncaring parenting will have a negative effect on children, but even the children of loving parents may develop in surprising ways. Parental communication, using body language and babble talk, is not a universal Esperanto but a language uniquely understood by each 'mother and baby' unit. A report published in 2009 in the journal *Current Biology* suggests that babies between three to five days old have 'cry melodies' which accord with their mother tongue. Early communication is an important stage in the bonding process and a precursor of later communication both with significant others and with long-term partners.

1

Careful Handling

Worldwide packaging and shipping.

Those who rely on the school bus each day will expect the driver to know the way. He has studied the Highway Code, passed an examination and been issued with a driving licence. But there are other drivers, other passengers, other journeys. These journeys start at birth. The 'drivers' think they are competent but they have had no instruction and the going may be hazardous. The drivers are parents and the passengers are children.

The passengers depend on the drivers and trust them. But some drivers may not have learned the unique mother/child language, the essence of bonding. They take chances, are careless, cause accidents or lose their way. The passengers may be bruised in transit. They will be damaged goods. Their trust has been misplaced and they have not been protected. Some become angry but are unable to direct their anger appropriately. They may turn it inwards and harm themselves, or outwards and harm others. Surrogate carers, child support agencies, the social services, the police, helplines and friends try to help them but can seldom provide little more than first-aid for the victims of those (parents) who took on a job for which they were not trained.

No licence is required for those who assume responsibility for the journey from childhood to adulthood. There are no health and safety rules, no instruction manuals, no compulsory (mental) health checks, no emotional MOTs. The immediate havoc caused by dangerous driving is obvious. But having to wait years to assess the damage caused by dangerous parenting throws the connection between the two out of focus. Parents have awesome responsibilities. One is to become aware of their power through thoughtful introspection and another is to encourage in their children a firm but friendly conscience. Introspection encourages the search for answers to questions seldom asked, while a friendly, rather than a harsh conscience, negates the frequent need to challenge it.

Clare, a twenty-six-year-old mother with a young baby with whom she was unable to bond, had an aversion to warm milk and also liked other drinks to be ice-cold. She asked herself what could have shaped this idiosyncratic need. Might this minor compulsion provide her with a clue to her mother's early nursery attitudes? Did she give her the cold shoulder, or perhaps the cold breast, when she needed something? She knew that her mother had never been particularly forthcoming. Was she unwittingly passing on to her own children a similar emotional frigidity?

Through introspection Clare gained insight into her behavioural habits and was put in touch with many of her emotional needs. It encouraged her not only to deal more appropriately with them but also helped her to avoid passing some of the less desirable aspects of her own childhood on to her baby. The emotionally deprived will not be particularly troubled by an aversion to warm milk, such as Clare experienced. But what if they understand that it is not so much the milk but its provider who was cold and unloving and that it was this that has led them to a compensatory attraction for chemicals, gambling, hypersexuality or repeated partner change? Realising that a cold upbringing may be the reason that they take drugs, they will not delude themselves that it is because of their effect, because their friends take them, or that they would be socially ostracised were they not to do so or to give them up. Neither will they claim that their addiction to risk-taking is harmless. They will realise that sex addiction is not a temporary variation in lifestyle necessary to help in the search for the right person, but a reaction to earlier emotional deprivation. The right person – the opposite sex parent who failed them – does not exist now because it did not exist then. When adults look for someone to understand them rather than someone with whom to share their lives they place themselves once again in the failed parent/child relationship.

Simon, the father of three young children, had been brought up to expect disappointment. His earliest memories were of his parents' invariable replies to requests. His mother would respond with 'Ask Daddy' and his father with 'I'll see'. Simon had little idea of what was meant since his father usually forget what it was he promised to look into. Simon became familiar with uncertainty. He grew up to be a pessimist. There was seldom anything pleasurable to look forward to. 'I'll see' became his response to his own children's requests. Simon was encouraged to rethink his habitual responses and unlike him his children were not denied the pleasures of joyful expectation.

In addition to the encouragement of introspection into their own upbringing, parental responsibility for the development of their child's conscience is equally important. Although genetic factors play a role (even if not one that cannot be modified) in social and moral behaviour, unnecessary and frequent disapproval of behaviour in a child which is irritating rather than bad, encourages the development of too condemning a conscience and an urge to challenge it later, rather than enjoying a friendly accommodation with it.

Children are taught how to distinguish between right and wrong at home and at school, but much more information is absorbed passively. Parents need to be seen to be acting appropriately. Dishonesty in minor matters – such as expressing pleasure when given too much change in a shop, or lying about a child's age when buying a ticket for a museum or cinema – feeds into a 'getting away with it attitude'. This is a small step perhaps towards 'getting away with murder' but a big step towards getting away with lesser, antisocial aspects of everyday life.

How many consider that their real addiction to chemicals or gambling or sex comes about because it briefly relieves the depressive mood caused by an upbringing punctuated by too many losses? Were they to do so might they then ask themselves what these losses are and how they might deal with them more appropriately?

Claude, a thirty-two-year-old guitarist in a rock band, whose mother had died in childbirth was brought up, an only child, by his doting father. Night after night in his lonely bedsitter Claude found himself becoming addicted to a virtual-reality computer game in which the player is asked to select an alternative lifestyle, career, marital status or gender. He chose to be a married woman, but it was a year before he realised that he was essentially gay. Realising that he had lost forever the opportunity of being close to a mother and by extension to women generally, he gave up the guitar to train for the more fulfilling career (for him) of hospital nurse.

Most parents, however unfamiliar they may be with the 'road ahead', do their best. If they take an idyllic view of their own childhood, they will bring up their children as they believe they were brought up. If they believe they were neglected they may over-compensate with their children and smother them, stifling and delaying their development. Occasionally parents intent on doing their best become overwhelmed by issues they had not anticipated.

Soon after her younger brother was born, three year-old Jane became increasingly preoccupied with her dolls. Her mother was pleased, since her new baby was taking up most of her time, and she knew that it was normal for small girls to play with dolls (their own babies). She hardly noticed that Jane's babies were being given plenty of loving attention. Neither did she consider that Jane might be telling her that she was also a baby and needed as much loving attention as her brother (and her dolls) was receiving. Jane was ignored. Her younger brother was picked up and fed as soon as he cried. One day Jane screamed at her brother to be quiet. Jane's behaviour became increasingly hostile to her brother and her mother became increasingly hostile to her.

Would Jane grow up with low self-esteem, believing she was unworthy of attention and have difficulty finding anyone to like her, or would she turn her anger in on herself and become depressed? Or would her mother, as soon as she sensed the problem, share the new baby with her daughter and work to restore her sense of worth? Even loved children may be greedily demanding. A wise mother will ask herself why her infants are dissatisfied. Does she have enough time for them, enough of the milk of human kindness? Does she try to understand their unspoken needs? Does she talk to them in a language of instinctual communication, initiating the bond between them that forms the basis of their identity? Or is she too self-conscious or too indifferent to indulge in babble talk, the first step towards close and loving communication. Adults who do not know the answer to the question 'Who am I' exist as chameleons, based on whoever or whatever they merge into at any given time. Believing they are no one unless they are someone else, and then only when they are with them, is a recipe for identity confusion. Mothers who are deaf to babble talk and blind to body language are pleased when their passive children seem happy to be left on their own. They should be displeased, because later as adults, uncertain as to their own identity, they will have difficulty in acknowledging the identity of others.

Good parents neither expect too much of their children nor delegate too many of their responsibilities to others. Good parents acknowledge and identify their children by looking at them and listening to them. Less good parents place their own unfulfilled needs before those of their children and may even look to them for compensation for what their own upbringing failed to provide. They may not recognise the factors in their parenting which influence their children's later lifestyle, but a close examination of the blueprint which informs their own choices will certainly enrich the lives of their children.

The traumas of childhood are never forgotten. If adults cannot recall them they will be compelled to repeat them. These repetitions (reflected in choice of career or leisure interests, sexual preferences or parenting style) are encrypted accounts of childhood. Decoding them is a revelation, the precursor to behavioural change.

Bad parents exploit children's fear of disapproval. A child's anger can be suppressed by the usual threats that 'Mummy won't love you if …' or 'Daddy will be angry when …' Children who fear that parental love will be withdrawn if they behave 'badly' are denied the right to express negative feelings. Rage, jealousy or envy are appropriate if, for example, a child is too young to understand that a newly arrived sibling has not in fact stolen attention which had previously been uniquely theirs – an issue that a sensitive parent would address. In the absence of such understanding, these children may later punish others for what they believe was done to them. If as adults however, they remember the emotional injury that caused their anger it will not be necessary to scapegoat others. Recollection does not come easily, but childhood traumas will be triggered when adults ask themselves why they do what they do.

The earliest memory of forty-year-old Philip whose attitudes to women were invariably hostile, was of being unable one morning at the age of three to push open his mother's (never before) locked bedroom door and to climb as usual into her bed. Many years later he realised the door was not closed against him because his mother had ceased to love him but because she was in labour. It was the birth of his sister not the bedroom door that had come between them.

Addressing his sensitivities at the time might have saved him from punishing other women for what he believed was his mother's earlier rejection.

Michael, a depressed and non-assertive ENT surgeon, dedicated his life to improving the hearing of others. He had however been passed over for promotion partly because he had never drawn attention to his achievements. No one had listened to him as a child and expecting that no one would listen to him as an adult he had failed to speak up for himself. Addressing his non-assertiveness and providing him with the insight needed to help him understand his career choice allowed him to promote his worth. It was too late however to help him listen more carefully to what his own children were saying when they were infants.

Compulsively repeated activities and thoughts provide clues to upbringing. Hostile reactions to those in authority, as well as gender prejudices, are more common in those whose fathering was deficient. Authority figures may be treated, consciously or unconsciously, with contempt or disapproval. Police and traffic wardens provoke loathing. One man whose interest in US government policy had hitherto been negligible became passionately anti-American when he heard America referred to as 'the world's policeman'. Men whose mothering was deficient may seduce women or look upon them as objects to be conquered or make distasteful demands of them. Women scorn men by robbing them of their potency or by turning away from them to other partners. If adults were not listened to as children, they may set up situations in which they cannot be heard such as interrupting the conversations of others because their childhood carers were deaf to their needs.

> Anna was surprised when it was pointed out to her that she seldom allowed her husband to finish a sentence. When she realised that by cutting him off in mid-stream she was in effect castrating him, in retaliation against her father who had abused her, she was able to overcome what had become over time a pattern of destructive behaviour. The relationship hitherto combative, rapidly improved.

Abused children may later adopt criminal behaviour to compensate for the wrongs done to them, but an apparently loved child may also be greedily demanding. Many mothers are pleased when their babies spend passive hours in their cradles gazing at the ceiling. They may not 'trouble' her, but may grow up to trouble others.

Ideal parents are those who live in harmony under the same roof and are readily available to their children. They neither expect too much of them nor delegate too many of their responsibilities for them. This is an absolute that can only rarely be achieved. Single parents and working mothers who are aware of their child's needs and conscious of the extra pressures to which they are exposed will provide appropriate, carefully monitored childcare back-up. Less than ideal parents focus on their own unfulfilled needs, often looking to their children to compensate them for what their own parents failed to provide. 'If you are good (to us) we will love you', instead of 'We love you because you are our children'.

Parental availability cannot be guaranteed when financial needs are pressing or marital breakdown threatens. In theses cases parents have a responsibility to ensure that their children are provided with trusted surrogates with whom they will feel safe.

Whether caring or exploitive, most parents believe that they act in the best interests of their offspring. If they rear angry children with poor self-esteem, these beliefs are incorrect. Parental influence, in the absence of unavoidable factors such as war, poverty and ill-health, is responsible for provoking the destructive as well as the creative potential of their children.

Most parents rely on their instincts and are fortunate if their children are easy to manage. A happy working alliance is formed. But what of the more difficult children, those who demand the unconditional love to which they are entitled, those who trouble parents? Will they grow up happy and contented or become misfits and dangerous? Will they wish they were someone else or somewhere else? And how might parents recognise these potential misfits and help them choose integration into the family and by extension into the community?

John, well known for his 'withering' put-downers, remembers at the age of eight cutting down a long row of standard roses in the garden that were his father's pride and joy. This 'phallic' attack on his rival for his mother's love was repeated as an adult in 'cutting' relationships with other men.

Had his mother realised that far from being destructive John was trying to make her understand that her love for his father should not exclude him, his legacy might have been less destructive.

If the hypothesis that infants are born innocent is assumed, then their subsequent behaviour will be shaped by the family environment in which they develop. If on the other hand it is believed that infants are born guilty and must work towards redemption then parents will need to provide them with all the help they can get.

Children know what they need. From birth onwards they have an uncontrollable hunger, first for food and security and later for information. Thoughtful parents will respond when their children want something or want to know something. They will also consider their children's behavioural inheritance.

Edward, whose adult life was ruled by the clock, suddenly realised at the age of thirty-four that his mother had for as long as he could remember kept him (and the rest of her family) waiting for meals. He had always known that this was not her intention but had never before realised that her unwitting timing problem had any effect on him. As an adult he knew that starting to eat before others were served was impolite but his anxiety levels were such that eating as soon as he was served had become an anxiety-reducing ritual that he was compelled to adopt. He knew that his behaviour hardly required a visit to a psychiatrist but that insight into its origins had made him wonder whether he might be passing it, and perhaps other behavioural anomalies, on to his children.

Thoughtless parents may tell their children to be quiet when others are speaking or when they are eating. Such niceties may be learned later by example rather than instruction. When children have something to say they need to say it. By delegitimising their hunger for food and information an unnatural inhibition is impressed upon them. Thoughtless parents will not have listened to their children, only to their own pre-formed agenda. Good might indirectly come of it but only for others. As advocates or as politicians where they are able to articulate the views of the silent majority they may grow up to help those who cannot speak for themselves. In addition to encouraging introspection in would-be parents, decoding habits of behaviour in children provides further insights.

Three year-old Leo would switch on all the lights in whatever room he found himself. His father, mindful of the electricity bill was opposed to this habit and his mother ignored it. Neither of them considered what it was that their son wished to shed light on or that it would be helpful to him to find out.

Was Leo bored? Did he need more input from them? Had they left him in the dark? Were they propelling him towards a life-long search for something that could never be found? They would only be able to think in these terms if they were aware that children 'act out' their thoughts and feelings because they are not old enough to speak them out. If they understood this they could then address their child's needs rather than condemning him to a life of aimless searching instead of one of productive research.

> Jeremy, five years old, not especially vocal, but fluent in body language, was asked by his mother to help her divide his toys into those he wanted to play with and those that could be disposed of. He understood that toys given away would be lost to him forever. He invariably chose to get rid of them. Was he saying to his mother that he was ready to move on because his past had been fulfilling and there was no need to hold on to it? Or was he saying that what she had given him was rubbish and that he could not wait to get rid of it? Further 'communication' would have provided the answer.

A compulsive need to repeat the traumas of childhood is inevitable; a search not for what is, but for what should have been. A child brought up in a hostile environment may, as an adult, look back in barely understood anger. One may be driven to become a historian, raking over battles long since lost. Another may become an archaeologist in the hope that by digging up the past he might find what had been hidden from him. A racing driver may spend his working life going round in circles on the track long before he asks himself why he is getting nowhere fast.

Those brought up in particularly insecure environments might be afraid to leave the safety of their homes. When they do they may search for the illusory 'securities' on offer in the financial services industry or be drawn into a relationship with another 'parent' who is likely to be as disappointing as their own. They have only to look in the mirror of compulsive repetition to see reflections not of themselves but of their past, providing them with the option of changing from the path chosen for them by their parents to one which they choose for themselves.

Parental influence, and to a lesser extent genetic predisposition and social circumstances, form a blueprint for the future. Lifestyle, nurturing behaviour, choice of emotional partner, appetite for sex and appetite for food as well as social factors – such as whether to go straight or take to crime – can all be found in this blueprint.

Children whose injustices have been addressed in a family setting – the ideal environment for the development of social conduct – are not likely to seek justice later by taking the law into their own hands. But parents, childminders and teachers often deny the important role they play in the overall psychological development of those entrusted to their care. Few would disagree however that an abused child might grow up to abuse others. But would most parents accept that the way they bring up their children will affect every other aspect of their later lives? The quality of the attachment between parents and newborn infants and the importance of recognising and responding to an infant's early signals requires extreme sensitivity. Inadequate parents have much to answer for. Their children will remain attached as they wait for the fulfilment denied them. When they do leave they are likely to re-enact, in one home after another, the injustices experienced in infancy leaving behind them a trail of antisocial distress.

Michael, a thirty-eight-year old British engineer, whose wife had died from cancer, fell in love with twenty-five-year old Yasmeen while he was working on a water project in India. Intent on marrying her he had at her family's insistence converted to Islam and then returned with his bride to the UK. Michael did not feel welcome on their occasional visits to his wife's family in India. Her brothers never addressed him directly but spoke to him only through their sister. Because they talked 'about' him rather than to him he felt excluded and his relationship with his wife began to suffer. He asked himself whether she could be trusted to continue loving him. Depressed, Michael sought professional help. In therapy he discovered the effect that his early life was having on him. His biological mother had been killed in a road accident soon after he was born. He was looked after by a nurse in a children's home until he was adopted by his mother's sister three months later. He had bonded with his mother, then with the nurse and later still with his aunt who had died when he was ten. Since the death of his wife he had not been able to make a commitment to any woman until he met Yasmeen.

He was encouraged to talk about the women who had loved him. Those who had committed to him – his mother briefly after his birth, the nurse and his adoptive mother and later still his wife – had all loved him and left him. He was eventually able to accept Yasmeen's family's reaction to him as nothing more than part of understandable bedding down and not a rejection. He was able to draw a line under a past that had been so influential and not blame Yasmeen for the interrupted parenting to which he had been exposed. He chose to stay married to her.

Good parenting is innate, probably on a scale of good enough to excellent. Some have it, others must acquire it. As with musicality, dexterity and sensitivity, it must be nurtured.

Thoughtful parents attempt to reverse the apparent indifference of their own parents by being tolerant and attentive with their children, tuning into and responding to their body language, discussing and debating issues with them when they are older and using instruction mainly to protect them from danger.

Punitive parents are strict with their children. They prefer at best the naughty step and at worst physical violence. No advocacy is involved and problems are more likely to be suppressed than discussed. Time-out from the family unit, if only to another room, is the equivalent to a child as a custodial sentence is to an adult. Only in situations where arousal levels in both parent and child are escalating and are accompanied by explanation can it be occasionally useful. Imprisoned offenders do not need to learn violent behaviour from other inmates (a common explanation for recidivism). They have already learned it from re-experiencing the restraints of an unhappy childhood. Punitive adults are encouraged by television programmes that feature behavioural training for 'naughty' children who are merely imitating the chaos they see around them. It might make for good television but is more suitable for dog training. Its entertainment level is on a par with other forms of 'reality TV' appealing to those who are amused by the discomfiture of others.

Promiscuous parents think wistfully of times past when drinking and 'going on the pull' were two of their major interests. They continue to indulge in excess and see little wrong in heavy drinking with friends while their children are in bed upstairs.

Bad parents abuse their children. Whether the abuse is emotional or physical it remains the commonest cause of pre-criminal and criminal behaviour. Personal choice, opportunity, inadequate education, poverty, low IQ, antisocial personality disorder, sub-standard housing, the male sex hormone, genes and gender, in the absence of good parenting will add to the mix. Chemical factors, including the low levels of the neurotransmitter serotonin sometimes found in depressives (associated with bouts of overwhelming and uncontrollable rage), the disinhibiting effect of alcohol and other drugs all contribute to inappropriate behaviour. Aware parents will do their best to mitigate their effects. Adults who understand why they have adopted their particular lifestyle will help their children not only make more fulfilling life changes for themselves but will also help them make better use of their talents. Good enough parents have nothing to answer for. From the beginning they will have been sensitive to their children's needs. When their children grow up and leave home their parenting job is done. They and their children will remain friends.

Cressida grew up in a family background in which her father in particular adored her. She considered her upbringing to have been a happy one and invariably described it as such to her friends. Yet there was an aspect of her adult behaviour that her father found puzzling. Whenever he telephoned her she would make an excuse to end the conversation quickly and tell him she would call him back. She seldom did. But when she made the call she would talk as long as was necessary.

Her father would ask himself why his otherwise affectionate daughter seemed to have no time for him. He recalled that she had a passion for watches, had asked him to give her one of his and treasured it (she wanted his 'time'). She was always in a hurry. Time was clearly important to her. Had he kept her waiting as a child? He remembered collecting her from her state school every day and although he knew that she welcomed this she also dreaded the other children's taunts about her father's expensive car (her friends went home on the bus). She could not wait to get this part of the day over with as quickly as possible. As an adult she had time for her father but only when she was in control of events. A more sensitive father might have realised that as a schoolgirl she was unable to do this. Had he done so, he would have been able to spare his daughter a painful outcome to what in the event was an unwitting trauma.

Parents have the power to shape the future. Most use this power benevolently. For reasons that range from failing to realise that they have this power, to their own inadequacies, to unavailability, or to the disharmony of divorce, a few parents do not do so. Their nurturing duties include understanding and interpreting their children's behavioural idiosyncrasies, providing them with security and a structured lifestyle, and the encouragement of moral values. In the absence of home care, children will seek distortions of such 'care' outside the home, hunting for it in gangs like hungry wolves. If parents recognise their nurturing duties and provide children with what they need, they will neither mourn the loss of it nor buy, steal, or kill for it later.

Some parents take comfort from the statistic that eighty-five per cent of child offenders grow out of criminality by the age of twenty-five. They should not. Considerable damage can be done to others before then. Most antisocial behaviour, ranging from violent crime to political extremism, is carried out by those under the age of twenty-five. Most are males. Females are catching up. Parents play a critical role.

Suicide bombing – an extreme behavioural anomaly ostensibly motivated by religious and/or political zealotry – is more likely to find recruits in those whose upbringing has failed them. Their passive/aggressive supporters use the bomber's stated motivation as a vehicle for their own prejudiced views. An adolescent who leaves home to prepare for a meeting with his heavenly father in the next world might suggest, amongst other things, that his earthly father had failed him in this one. Returning to a violence which denied them justice when they were infants, failed them then as its repetition does now. It is hardly likely that those, whose crimes range from theft and murder, to threatening the human rights of others, will have come from homes where their own human rights were scrupulously observed.

Paradoxes exist. Destiny and destination are intertwined. Most think of destiny as something they can do nothing about. Providence and fate. What will be will be. A philosophy left to play itself out rather than a game plan. Small children think neither of destiny nor destination. Their destination is certain. It may arrive early through illness, accident or neglect, unwittingly through parents whose inexperience conceals dangers, or later by good fortune, good genes or good parenting. Considerable thought, effort and expense are spent in finding ways of postponing the arrival at their destination through treating and preventing physical and mental illness more effectively. Less thought, effort and expense are spent in helping parents understand the importance of their role in determining their children's quality of life.

Rosalind was an attractive thirty-year-old unmarried art historian. Her earliest memory was of her baby brother's christening when she was four. She remembers being taken out of the church because she was crying. 'I was outside and all the others were inside.' Her core problem as an adult, her apparent destiny, was her sense of isolation, of not belonging either to her family or to any other group. She had put these feelings down to the shape of her nose (which was of normal appearance) for which she wanted cosmetic surgery. Her life-long role of 'outsider' was not because of her appearance which she believed could be remedied by surgery but because she had been 'excommunicated' from the church (the Holy Family) at the age of four.

The destinies of both parents and their children are determined by their interactions with one another. Unlike the highly valued 'good baby' who seldom cries, who demands little and receives little and grows up to seek compensatory attention, the 'bad baby' demands much, receives much and probably grows up more fulfilled. How little input is required to stimulate the driving ambition that leads an emotionally hungry, talented baby to grow up to become a captain of industry or a Nobel laureate? How much input does a 'bad' baby with problematic genes need to avoid a future so bereft that criminal compensation for it is sought? The fine line between a rocket and a damp squib, between a genius and a delinquent, between a depressive and a suicide bomber, echoes the difference between the good enough parent and the not good enough parent.

Parents learn their parenting skills from their parents and from their children. Good parents pass on good skills; bad parents pass on bad ones. Relying on passively acquired learning stimulated by their children's responses to them, may emphasise the benefits of instinctive nurturing, but it cannot match the benefits gained by actively learning to decode the behavioural patterns of those whose upbringing is shaping not only their careers, but their leisure interests, their political views and their sexual preferences.

Nowhere is this more important than the role such decoding plays in understanding the causes of crime. Since every aspect of criminal behaviour accurately reflects the details of the failed parent/child interaction, throwing light on the information within that interaction could, in one generation, even in the absence of professional therapeutic intervention, be more helpful in reducing the incidence of crime than intervening once crime has occurred. Choosing rectitude rather than criminality, like choosing one's parents, is a non-starter. Understanding one's upbringing is not only easier but essential.

2

Parental Responsibility

Children begin by loving their parents. After a time they judge them. Rarely if ever do they forgive them.

Oscar Wilde

Several options are available to children on receipt of their gift. 'Take it or leave it' is a passive option accepted by most children, at least until they leave home when they may then switch to a more active 'resentment' option. This may lead to an increase in antisocial behaviour blamed usually on parents who work, by other parents who work, but whose (usually financial) circumstances allow them to continue with their chosen lifestyle.

'Making the best of it' is another option, usually more socially acceptable, but which makes no allowance for children whose lifestyle does not emotionally fulfil them. The 'gratitude' option, available mainly to those who have experienced concerned parenting, is the only option unlikely to lead to antisocial behaviour.

When antisocial behaviour arises out of the resentment option, government ministers (mainly male) pledge to step up their fight against yob culture by 'hitting them where it hurts', banning offenders from attending football matches or from taking holidays abroad. Zero tolerance on policing, providing more prisons and increasing the number and severity of antisocial behaviour orders (ASBOs) are popular mainly with the politically self-righteous. Politicians, elected by punitive parents (actual or potential) to speak for them, insist that they alone should set sentencing guidelines. The judiciary however, working to a different agenda, announced plans (ostensibly to free up more space in overcrowded prisons) for murderers to serve a minimum of ten years (instead of fifteen) and prison sentences for burglars to be cut by a quarter.

Teachers, more in touch with parenting issues, come closest to understanding who is to blame for the high levels of crime. Addressing the National Association of Head Teachers annual conference in May 2004, its General Secretary David Hart agreed that 'inadequate parenting bears [some] responsibility for crime,' adding: 'It has long been known that children with an antisocial or abusive parent are more likely to grow up to violate the rights of others'. No one spelled out what 'inadequate parenting' meant or what steps should be taken to help parents understand what it meant. Nevertheless in 2004 the minister for children, in a consultation paper on youth, proposed offering parents courses in how to improve family life. Advice would be given on disciplining children and how to deal with sex, drugs and bullying. Encouraging parents to look at their own behaviour was not on the agenda. By 2006 the number of ASBOs was so high that it was difficult for either the police or the courts to deal with them. Over fifty per cent of offenders breached them and many flaunted them as if they were decorations of honour rather than badges of shame. Comments about the offenders such as 'They have no respect for the law or for their parents' were common. Comments that their parents might have had 'no respect for their children' were absent.

The question of 'parental responsibility', a term used in the 1989 Children's Act began to be addressed in July 2004. During a debate in the House of Lords on the Children Bill the Attorney-General Lord Goldsmith, wanted the law on smacking children updated from the nineteenth-century 'Reasonable Chastisement', to permitting only a 'gentle tap'. Lord Lester of Herne Hill suggested an amendment that permitted smacking only if it did not harm children 'mentally as well as physically'. Was he concerned that the long-term mental effect of inflicting pain on the buttocks followed by a warm embrace, might eroticise the buttocks and introduce the concept of violence as a component of 'love' in later life? Sexual pleasure derived from inflicting pain may be at the root of much adult violence. It probably also accounts for the use of torture in closed institutions – detention centres, prisons, the armed services and schools – as well as to the over-emphasis on pain at the expense of affection in 'spanking' during foreplay. Lord Lester's amendment was more pertinent than he may have realised.

During the Commons debate, David Hinchcliffe (Labour) introduced a clause that would give children the same rights as adults against assault. He told the House that 'it was a scandal that in twenty-first-century Britain one child every week dies at the hands of their parents or carers'. He could have added that it was equally scandalous that somewhere in the world parents die, perhaps every minute, at the hands of other people's children (adult in body but not in mind) seeking retribution for bad parenting by taking the law into their own hands.

King George V's frequently quoted comment that 'he had been afraid of his father and by God his children would be afraid of him' encapsulates not only what was wrong with the House of Windsor in the early twentieth century, but what is still wrong a hundred years later in families where hitting [helpless] children continues to be recommended.

Violence can never be an answer. In the enclosed environment of a prison cell, violence may be sexually gratifying for the perpetrator. For the victim it mirrors an earlier 'torture chamber', an encounter between a helpless infant and a maternal oppressor. If what should have been a pleasant quasi-sexual (mouth/breast) experience was not, the victim, satisfying a sadistic need for retaliation might later redress the balance by inflicting pain (often sexual) on a scapegoat.

The major concern of a mother on maternity leave is with the emotional well-being of her child. A father, having to return to work will be more involved with the provision of material security for his family. Their joint wish for a loving ongoing 'hands-on' approach to child-rearing may be thwarted by the need to share this with surrogates.

For mothers, emancipation in the workplace once gained cannot be casually abandoned. Yet even those in full-time employment cannot delegate all responsibility for their children to others. The tendency for women to delay childbirth until they have proved their professional competence puts them into an unwanted double bind. It is hard to give up a career passionately worked for; but neither can long-awaited pregnancies with their due rewards be easily set aside. State funding leaves both mother and child only partially fulfilled.

A return to work before the completion of the bonding process may lead to feelings of guilt in the mother and/or behavioural problems in the child.

Two weeks of paid paternity leave (with some discussion about whether the taxpayer or the employer should pay for an extension) is a poor reward for equally poor services rendered by fathers. Their role in child-rearing is important in the prevention of violent crime. However in a survey carried out by the Chartered Institute of Personnel and Development in 2004 sixty per cent of men and women felt that the current level of paternity leave was about right. Most men seem to support a work culture which will make them feel guilty if they take off too much time (but not if they remain at home helping their partners cope with their newborn infant). In 2003 only one in five fathers opted to take their statutory two-week allowance.

Both parents are obliged to spend much of their time at work fulfilling their material needs, rather than at home fulfilling their children's emotional ones. Despite financial pressures however, many women dread the time when maternity leave ends, and their babies are left in the care of others.

Today family units have adjusted to two salaries. Money – like food, sex, alcohol, drugs and religion – has become an addictive token. Although parents may be aroused by prosperity, infants are aroused by parents. Few parents want to return to the time when the family's finances were managed by one of them and the home by the other. The need to support more than a minimalist lifestyle often means that both must seek work outside the home. Parents convince themselves that taking maternity leave will provide their children with sufficient love and security to ensure that they will not turn to an inappropriate lifestyle later. All other things being equal they may be right. But sometimes they are wrong.

When their emotional needs are withheld, children risk growing up with a compulsion to seek compensation in ways which mirror the type of neglect to which they were exposed by their parents. By examining their own patterns of behaviour, choice of career, leisure interests, sexual preferences, political beliefs and any lifestyle activity to which they are compulsively and passionately attached, prospective and actual, parents will recognise reflections of their own upbringing. In so doing they will better understand their responsibilities to their children.

> Eight-year-old Ross, an only child, like many thousands of other evacuees during World War Two was sent to the United States under the care of his mother's sister. His aunt tried to integrate him into her large family but Ross resented being a cuckoo in the nest and failed to adapt. It was almost four years before he was restored both to his parents and to his status of only child. He returned to his old school, comforted to discover that many of his friends had undergone experiences similar to his own. He completed his education and went to university. Once again his suppressed resentment at being 'abandoned' took a form that was to persist throughout his adult life. He developed a compulsive need to seek approval from women, while at the same time punishing them for his mother's earlier rejection. Disappointing women never completely satisfied his need for revenge and therefore needed to be continually repeated. Not having been particularly close to his father led merely to a weak anti-authoritarian bias which took the form of a contemptuous devaluation of the views expressed by his male friends.

Those who feel that they have not been loved enough as children will seek reassurances that they are lovable as adults. When reassurance is not immediately available some will overeat or seek 'love' chemically, some will buy it, and others may steal it. Ross essentially stole it. Those who believe that wealth symbolises security, may devote their lives to its acquisition in the mistaken belief that money can buy them love. By re-enacting their unfulfilled nursery needs both in their sexual fantasies and in reality, they hope that they will be afforded a second chance to satisfy their hitherto thwarted desires.

By learning how to look at their childhood, potential parents will discover what they must do to save their children from the problems they have themselves faced. An increasing number of adults have indicated that they are ready to look at the past, whether collective or individual. This is confirmed by the number of hits on genealogy websites, which in 2006 were second only to pornography ones. It is only a small step from wanting to know where one's antecedents lived and worked to how their mothers interacted with them in the nursery.

Maternal rejection may be publicly signalled by those suffering from it. The 'builder's bum', a symbolic 'turning one's back' message, far from being erotic is quite likely to signal an unhappy, turned away from, childhood. Increasing numbers of girls no longer walk hand in hand with boys but hand in back pocket with them. If the buttock replaces the breast as a nurturing token – a role that biologically it obviously cannot play – the breast is denigrated from its feeding function to one of waste and disposal.

Embezzlement by an adult draws attention to the insecure child within. Embezzlers delude themselves that they have a 'right' to the money they steal but it is only an infant who has a right to both his mother's milk and her love. If he is denied this right the unloved child may claim the right to other assets that clearly do not belong to him. He will then be charged with fraud, despite his belief, often delusional in its intensity, that he is innocent of criminal intent. His mother was also innocent of criminal intent but she may have been guilty of failing to tune in to her child's earliest needs.

> Oscar, a sixty-year-old married man of unchallenged probity, has a clear memory as an only child, of helping himself, between the ages of seven and ten, to money from his mother's purse. He recalls no feeling of wrongdoing. It was only much later as an adult that he asked himself why, if his mother's most valued gift was her love for him, was it necessary for him to steal it?

In late 2003 some of the financial officers and executives of Parmalat (the Italian multinational food giant), whose major products are milk and yoghurt, were charged with a multibillion euro fraud. Calisto Tanzi the founder of the firm was arrested and detained in Milan's San Vittore jail. His request to be held under house arrest (the usual location for the grounded child) was refused by the magistrate who failed to understand why the profits derived from the vast quantities of milk traded by his company had not satisfied him.

_eprived infant remains addicted to symbolic versions of his mother's major asset, her milk. Children may seek to satisfy their addiction to gratification through high arousal activities such as sexual promiscuity, illicit drugs, risk-taking, or by bingeing on food or alcohol. But it is only much later that they discover that the milk they so longed for in infancy has turned sour, and like Calisto Tanzi's yoghurt, become a poisoned chalice.

> Thirty-year-old Rupert was an only child brought up by his widowed mother and a nanny. He took second place to his mother's business interests and to her social life. He saw little of her as a small child and even less after he was sent to boarding school at the age of eight. He remembers her only as being secretive and withholding. On leaving school he was keen to enter the family textile business because he thought it might at last bring the mother he adored closer to him. This did not happen. She grudgingly acknowledged him as the heir to the family fortune but refused to share business decisions with him. She remained a non-giver as she had been in his childhood. Time passed and his mother retired although she continued to draw a high income from the business. Rupert was depressed and lonely. He turned to the casino for comfort. Within two years he had lost all his money at the tables and, to his great satisfaction, most of his mother's also.

The symbolism of his choice of game, blackjack, was lost on him. Was he the black knave, and the décolleté dealer a longed-for lady bountiful? The casino was happy to indulge him. Since he was a heavy and persistent loser they allowed him to set the scene of his own downfall. The dealer had to be a woman, close but out of reach, and the table had to be a private one. No one was permitted to use it while Rupert was playing (as an only child he had no experience of sharing his mother with anyone). A full glass of milk, untouched, was always at his side, a reminder both of the mother whose assets he was steadily destroying and – like Calisto Tanzi's yoghurt – the poisoned chalice of his childhood.

Feeding problems in infancy and the maternal frustrations linked to them may have a considerable knock-on effect on the infant. Greedy and over-demanding in all aspects of their lives, the deprived constantly seek gratification, affection and attention. Even those who do not consider themselves deprived may be seen with companions 'stolen' from other marital units. Insisting on immediate service in restaurants, they will return their food on the specious grounds that it was (as in their infancy) not to their taste. Their constant need for 'more' encourages them to conceal the full extent of their income from the tax inspector, to make fraudulent insurance claims and for 'expenses', and to demand free upgrades from the airlines.

Others who are deprived and who as adults abuse drugs rarely examine the reasons why they have a compulsive need to seek the comfort of chemicals. According to statistics published by police and health agencies, in 2000 and 2001 as many as one in fifty thirty- to forty-four-year-olds injected crack cocaine and heroin. If they do not understand their anger at having been discriminated against in infancy, they themselves will become victims of it, turning their anger inwards and damaging their physical and mental well-being. Those bent on revenge seek out innocent scapegoats as stand-ins for their apparently neglectful parents.

When males who have had problems with their mothers opt for a life of crime their crimes are likely to have sexual meaning. The uninvited invasion of another person's space is forcible entry. Men, as well as women may feel as if they have been raped when their homes have been broken into. They are unlikely to be impressed by the fact that the intruder is really an emotionally hungry small boy looking for love.

Women who have had poor relationships with their mothers might also turn to crimes with sexual content. In stealing their friend's husbands or adopting hidden violence as in binge eating followed by vomiting, they express contempt for the mothers who once fed them. Others may passively collude with a violent male partner in his sexual crime. In the past women were less often physically violent because their male hormone levels are lower than those of men. Physical violence in adolescent girls due probably to lack of social inhibition and despite lower hormone levels is now approaching the male level.

Ian Huntley, paradoxically a school caretaker, was jailed for life for the murder of two ten-year-old girls, Holly Wells and Jessica Chapman, in the village of Soham in Cambridgeshire in 2003. He had scapegoated and punished not one but two loving mothers by depriving them of their children. His girlfriend, Maxine Carr, whose own need for loving attention prevented her from recognising her envy of the love that Holly and Jessica had clearly been given by their parents colluded in their murder by lying to protect her partner. She was sentenced to three and a half years in jail for perverting the course of justice. When she was released she was given a new identity and provided with a safe house to protect her from other victims of abusive childhoods ever ready to revenge themselves on fraudulent care-givers.

Most crimes are gender related. Breaking and entering has always been essentially a male offence. A woman was until recently considered to be seldom sufficiently aggressive to be involved in anything other than fraud, petty theft such as shoplifting, or aspects of drug-related crime. Burglary, like rape, is an illicit bid for potency by the powerless. Theft is not the only motivation. Burglars, like rapists, take pleasure in humiliating their victims. They sometimes urinate and defecate onto furniture and carpets like incontinent infants and wantonly damage the homes they have violated, unconsciously avenging an earlier home which their unconscious tells them has damaged them. Housebreaking may not necessarily be sexually gratifying, but it can be highly arousing. Overt sexual and violent activity is often carried out as part of the criminal act, using the helpless and the elderly as scapegoats for unfulfilling parenting.

By 2004 there was widespread support for a change in the law which would permit householders to use force against intruders. The jailing of a Norfolk farmer, for killing a teenage burglar two years earlier aroused such retaliatory rage in other victims that a BBC opinion poll indicated that a majority would be prepared to take up arms to protect themselves against anyone intent on violating their 'space'. A few months later, another judge, presumably more in tune with the angry parent, ruled that a farmer who had shot a burglar who had broken into his home on three occasions 'could not be criticised' for the way he had defended his property.

Joyriding may be used by an adolescent male to provide him with at least an illusion of the power and potency to which he aspires, having probably never recovered from the childhood struggle with his father for his mother's love. By stealing and misusing a car, he feels he has acquired a status which he hopes will compensate him for his moral impotence, boost his self-esteem, and impress his peer group. The girl who goes along for the ride is herself contaminated by her boyfriend's hypersexuality. Playing with another man's phallic pride will give the joyrider a masturbatory, self-gratifying, non-transactional, same-sex fulfilment. Deluding himself that he owns the vehicle which he believes will highlight and enhance his virility, the youth who breaks into a car has the same motivation as the housebreaker. Those who are satisfied with contemptuously scoring a car's paintwork devalue an anonymous rival's symbol of power by acting out their phallic envy.

A youth with more transactional sexual ambitions may snatch a woman's bag, taking from it not only her possessions but her virtue (symbolically concealed within it). The fact that a man has had his hand in her bag/womb provokes in a woman a response disproportionate to the actual loss. Although she may in fact have lost her keys (to her privacy), her money, and her credit cards (to her security), and even her tampons (an unhappy association), what she may feel that she has actually lost is her integrity. The perpetrator may feel that he has gained a victory in his struggle for his mother's love. Some victims may respond more pragmatically. The absence of an emotional response in a woman might indicate a lack of femininity, while an emotional response in a man who has had his pocket picked, might suggest that he is gay.

A hostage-taker tests his own worth against that of his hostage. Ransom money will be some compensation for the emotional riches he has been denied. Envying what he believes to be the happy and secure background of his prisoner, he hopes that by stealing a child from his home, attention will be paid to him. Media silence thwarts this aim. Seeing aspects of himself in his victim, the kidnapper's behaviour may alternate between caring understanding, and the re-enactment of jealousy once directed towards a preferred sibling. Hostage-taking, like other acts of terrorism, provides criminals with high levels of arousal and fulfilment. A political hostage-taker believes that the group he embraces (and which he hopes embraces him) is an alternative family. Promised freedom from a tyrant (his father) and the approval of his peer group (his siblings), he pursues his aims with the single-minded behaviour of the deprived child. The defenceless hostage becomes increasingly at one with his captor. Now reduced to the helplessness of a child, he tries to please those in authority over him, knowing that he cannot survive without their 'love'. It may be years before he realises that this love was exploitive.

Terry Waite, the Archbishop of Canterbury's special envoy to the Middle East in 1987, was captured by Arab terrorists. Despite his five-year ordeal during which he was chained to a radiator, beaten, kept in solitary confinement for four years, subjected to mock executions to amuse his captors and transported from one prison to another in a giant fridge, his resolve, despite his physical helplessness, was reinforced by his Christian faith, characterised by his belief in the Holy Family who would never let him down. He later tried to return to Lebanon, in order to forgive those who had kidnapped him. On 11 September 2001 ten years after his release, terrorists committed the worst single attack of mass terrorism yet seen when two highjacked aircraft were deliberately flown into the twin towers of New York's World Trade Centre. On 23 January 2002 Terry Waite's comment that 'he could recognise the conditions that prisoners were being kept in at Guantanamo Bay' and that his fear that the US government was more concerned with revenge than justice suggests that identification with his captors was still paramount.

The comments made by the families of suicide bombers are often similar. They are based on the parental observation that their son (or daughter) would not hurt a fly. Did their child suffer from the 'good baby' syndrome? Quiet, well-behaved babies who grow up believing that they were loved because they were quiet may one day 'explode'. When a spiritual leader, claiming to speak on behalf of a heavenly father, offers a child the certainty of massive loving input in the next world and also the opportunity to express long-suppressed angry feelings towards mothers and other children for having been ignored in this one, it is an offer some may be persuaded to accept. Parents should welcome demanding babies who never bottle up their feelings, always make their presence felt and as a result receive the attention to which they are entitled, not because of their behaviour, but because they exist.

The armed rapist, who holds the life of his victim in his hands, resembles both the hostage-taker and the suicide bomber. His potency is so exaggeratedly enhanced by his grandiosity and omnipotence that sexual activity with his victim, far in excess of his usual pattern, may continue despite repeated ejaculation. The illusion of power and control achieved by the conquest of a woman both motivates and excites him. Mastery of the situation is of prime importance. His behaviour is unpredictable since he will be responding to fantasies of which his victim is unaware. Reasoned discussion with the hyperactive is occasionally effective, but it is unlikely to be successful when one player holds – and conceals – all the cards. At the moment of his crime a rapist believes that he is 'as God' and has at his mercy a scapegoat for parents who withheld attention from him because as a baby he either seldom asked for it or if he did no one responded.

All high-risk crime evokes massive levels of arousal. This has an effect on the criminal similar to that of alcohol, or other mood enhancing drugs on the depressed, the emotionally deprived and the sexually impotent. The criminal is often prey to all these conditions and his victim (whom he expects to compensate him for his early losses) is helpless in his hands. The essentially powerless, when they possess power, temporarily, remain in an overactive and highly disturbed state for some time. Hyperarousal leads to increasingly uncontrolled behaviour. This is associated with the disinhibition, brought about by the stimulation of the body's own chemistry evoked by the excitement of risk-taking, to which the risk-taker becomes addicted. The sex criminal's arousal levels are particularly intense leading to a sense of fulfilment seldom before experienced.

Serial killing with sexual motivation first became recognised when the serial murderer, known only as Jack the Ripper, hit the headlines in 1888. Until that time it was thought that murder generally was carried out for motives such as money or revenge, or during a drunken brawl. Jack the Ripper, barely aware of the evil in himself may have uniquely convinced himself that he had a divine mission to punish evil in others. On the morning of 31 August 1888, a prostitute was found with her throat cut and an incision made in her abdominal wall. Four other women were similarly murdered over the following ten weeks. The murders then ended as abruptly as they had begun. Although no sexual activity had actually taken place, the Ripper's attacks were nonetheless designated sex murders.

In every case the Ripper's intentions seemed to have been the defeminisation of his victims whose features were defaced and crude attempts made to excise their uteruses. What more certain way to ensure a woman's infertility (an echo perhaps of the murderer's jealousy of a sibling) than to carry out a hysterectomy on her?

Did the Ripper choose prostitutes because he believed his mother was promiscuous with her love? Were they scapegoats – not for an unfaithful wife or mistress – but for a mother who had neglected him in the interests of her own sexual needs? The concept of scapegoating was not clearly understood until Sigmund Freud drew attention to it and such motivation for the Ripper's pre-Freudian acts of vengeance would be unlikely to have been considered by the police at the time.

Supposition about the identity of the Ripper has ranged from a surgeon at the nearby London Hospital, via an émigré Russian doctor, the artist Walter Sickert, to the Duke of Clarence (the older brother of Prince George, subsequently King George V) who until his premature death at the age of twenty-six was heir to the British throne. A medical man no matter how inept could not possibly have made such a botched job of a straightforward surgical procedure such as a hysterectomy, and the Duke of Clarence worshipped his mother and was unlikely to have been intimately involved with or even interested in a woman's sexuality. Only Walter Sickert has remained a suspect. Were his early twentieth-century paintings of prostitutes anxiety-reducing confessionals or were they merely an attempt to enter the mind of a murderer whose motives fascinated him? The murders ended abruptly on 9 November 1888. The violent Ripper, possibly finding the evil within him impossible to live with, is thought by some to have killed himself.

Crimes of passion always had a place in the criminal records but the deliberate murder of a number of women all probably unknown to the murderer was something new. There have since been serial killers whose crimes have been equally gruesome. Jack the Ripper was the first to capture the public imagination. Not only were the murders notable for introducing the concept of serial killing to newspaper readers, they also indicated to subsequent murderers that until they were apprehended they would create a degree of terror in the public which would of itself be gratifying. Within three years the killing of the prostitutes was followed by a number of copy-cat murders. Some killers sought to justify their behaviour by appealing to the public conscience. Frederick Deeming (who was hanged in 1892 and deluded himself that he was performing a service to society rather than revenging himself on a neglectful mother) cemented the bodies of several prostitutes under the kitchen floor, insisting that they were 'spreading a vile infection'. In the same year Doctor Thomas Neil Cream, an American back-street abortionist living in London, was so offended by the behaviour of his prostitute victims, that he punished them by poisoning them with strychnine so that they would have a slow and painful death. He, like Frederick Deeming, was also hanged in 1892. His last words were: 'I am Jack ...'

In January 2000, more than a century later, Dr Harold Shipman a general practitioner, formerly addicted to pethidine and a prolific serial killer is thought to have murdered, by lethal injection, well over 250 of his patients. In one six-year period alone in which he had killed 143 people he had illegally obtained more than 24,000 milligrams of heroin. Most of his victims were female and many of them were old enough to have been his mother. He was sentenced to life imprisonment at Preston Crown Court but was found hanged in his cell in Wakefield Prison in 2004 taking with him, if not to his grave, but at least to a Sheffield mortuary, the reasons for his crime. Nothing is known of Harold Shipman's past other than that his mother died from cancer at the age of forty-two when he was taking his A-levels. Was he so affected by her suffering that he resolved that whenever possible he would ease the passing of other mothers or had she so failed him during his childhood that serially scapegoating other mothers became the only outlet for his anger?

At any rate, his own wife, to whom he had been married for thirty-seven years, who had worked with him as a part-time receptionist and who visited him weekly in prison until his death, as well as his four children, thought of him as an exemplary husband and father. Clearly loving and respecting his wife and children (his family could not believe that he had killed himself and were convinced that he had been murdered), his hostility to women had to be dealt with elsewhere.

There have been crimes in which sex has been the motive and other crimes where the power component has been a sufficient incentive. The sexually inadequate and hostile male, sometimes confused as to his true sexual orientation and likely to have been brought up in the absence of affectionate feelings has much to gain from the illusion of power achieved by frightening other people's mothers. The press bears some responsibility for this. Their claim that they have a duty both to inform and to warn the public of danger is reinforced by readers, usually women, who want to be kept informed about escaped prisoners and local crime. No woman is likely to benefit from knowing that a rapist is at large in her area however, unless she is prepared to barricade herself in her home until he is caught. Were numbers of women known to do this, those motivated by an overwhelming urge to exert power over women might be further encouraged.

As the criminal grows increasingly addicted to the chemistry of arousal, omnipotent defences against his inadequate personality become apparent. He is compelled to repeat his crime because, like other addicts, he is unable to cope with the withdrawal symptoms. In an interview shown on television in 1993 this was confirmed by the homosexual serial killer Dennis Nilsen ten years after he had been convicted of murdering sixteen young men, dismembering their bodies, and burying them beneath the floorboards in his house. Nilsen, like most men, whether heterosexual or homosexual, was homophobic. He was unable to tolerate rejection by men. Providing men accepted his sexual overtures – thus reassuring him of his potency – he felt at one with them. In a letter to his only surviving victim, Carl Stotter, a former dancer, Nilsen wrote: 'No one who slept with me died. Once someone had established his homosexual identity, then (my) control returned.' Nilsen's need to assert sexual power over his victims was exactly equal and opposite to his fear of their sexual power over him. He illustrated this point during his TV interview by commenting that 'the most exciting part of the little conundrum was when I lifted the body with its limp limbs dangling and carried it. It was an expression of my power to lift and carry and have control. The more obviously passive the victim the more powerful I was'. Clearly what he was unable to tolerate in men was the erect penis in its symbolic form, as thrust, power and strength. As a child he would have seen his father as powerful and threatening. As an adult he would have sought revenge by demonstrating his own power. When the penis represented love he desired it; when it was limp he felt rejected by it and it then became the stimulus for murder. Through his violent and murderous rage, Nilsen was probably saying that in his upbringing there was a man whom he feared would kill him, a man who clearly did not love him. Were the men he murdered scapegoats for this man, his father?

The key to the behaviour of Peter Sutcliffe, the Yorkshire Ripper, another serial murderer, may lie in a comment he made in a letter to a pen friend in which he claimed that he had persuaded media personality Sir Jimmy Savile to make a donation of £500 to dying and underprivileged children. The picture of himself that he sends to those who ask him for a photograph, is one that he says makes him look like Jesus Christ. He sees himself not only as omnipotent but also as a martyr who, unlike Jesus, suffered not for the sins of others, but perhaps for those of his parents. Sutcliffe, like the original Ripper, set out to murder women. He killed thirteen and attacked seven others. He was jailed in 1981 having been given twenty life sentences. Sutcliffe had roamed the red light district of Leeds's Chapeltown in search of victims, much as Jack the Ripper had roamed London's East End. He was concerned as much with competing with, and taunting the police, as he was with sexual gratification or the punishment of women.

The legacy of a childhood in which the overwhelming power of authority leads to a later omnipotent wish to achieve power over authority, is one feature at least of the bitter inheritance of a serial killer's upbringing. Sutcliffe left another legacy to the son of one of his victims. Almost thirty years after the Yorkshire Ripper murdered his first victim, Wilma McCann, her son Richard published his autobiography. In it he described an upbringing with a physically abusive father and a mother whom he knew loved him, but who had been taken from him when he was five. He described growing up bruised mentally and physically and as an adult sought comfort in sex and drugs. Later in therapy he learned to confront his past and draw a line under it. Richard acquired parenting skills through an understanding of the patterns of behaviour forced upon him, leaving him free to make whatever changes he felt appropriate.

David Canter, Professor of Psychology at the University of Surrey, has said that sex killers may often be former police officers or have had army careers. He believes that they will have been drawn to these occupations because they identify with over-strict fathers rather than wishing to punish recalcitrant mothers. He believes that their fathers were their role models but they later rebelled against them and against authority in general. Other psychologists believe that criminals copy the techniques of other criminals whom they admire and who become their heroes.

Offender profiling is used in an attempt to gain convictions in sex crimes. Police believe that certain criminals are obsessed with taunting them in a desire to outwit them. Such criminals play a complex game which they are determined to win and are delighted when the police, to reassure themselves that they are up against no ordinary lawbreaker, attribute qualities to them such as intelligence and resourcefulness. Flattered by this admiration, the criminal is encouraged to repeat his crime in order to live up to what he believes is both the police and the public's expectation of him.

Giving nicknames to such criminals increases their feelings of grandiosity. They may be encouraged to repeat their challenge to authority feeding into their ever increasing need for arousal enhanced by reading accounts of their exploits in the press. By regularly reporting the frustration of the police, the newspapers fuel the killer's grandiose need for stimulation and encourage the repetition of the behaviour that provides him with it. Press silence would cut off this source of satisfaction. It is argued that the criminal might then be encouraged either to take risks in order to satisfy his need for excitement, or be panicked into other aspects of high profile behaviour – talking in pubs or boasting to friends – thereby providing the police with much-needed information.

Crime as 'entertainment' has never been more popular, presumably mainly with those who see aspects of their own background in them. The material ranges from the apparently innocuous *Crimewatch UK*, an informative TV programme providing a public service (which is nonetheless presented with an eye to ratings), to sexually sadistic and morally deviant films. Magazines such as *Real Life Crimes* describe recent murders, with accompanying pictures and have a weekly circulation of 300,000 copies. In 1994, reality TV, a new form of entertainment was introduced to cable and satellite TV viewers who accompanied the emergency services into violent battle zones in which they could choose to identify with either the police or the criminal.

Bad behaviour in others has a fascination for those whose own bad behaviour is only tenuously under control. *Celebrity Big Brother* in which the nuts and bolts of day-to-day interactions are overheated by the enclosed environment in which they occur, has high ratings. John Humphrys (Radio 4 *Today* programme presenter) giving the annual MacTaggart Lecture at the Edinburgh Television Festival (2004) said that reality television 'demeans us all' and is 'undeserving of the name'. He also condemned as 'aggressive and violent' soaps such as *Coronation Street* and *EastEnders* mainly watched by lonely adults whose childhoods were presumably spent as observers of a family life in which they played little part, and by children who are attracted to programmes which glamorise and legitimise bad behaviour.

Although the law-abiding majority is both terrified and fascinated by violence, by confronting their fears at a safe distance, either in print or on the screen, they become more informed. The criminal minority however, similarly exposed to these images, become desensitised and as a result more callous. As the internet replaces television as a major source of pornographic violence against women, most people believe that laws against internet obscenity should be more vigorously enforced. Research published by the Broadcasting Standards Council revealed that most people were appalled by the ITV interview with Dennis Nilsen (1993), and they also found television reconstructions of other violent crimes distressing. These are the views of the non-criminal majority, but what of the effect on the criminal minority? Given the correct mix of predisposing factors to crime, such as disturbed personality, genetic factors, chemical facilitators such as alcohol or drugs superimposed over a traumatic childhood, horrific visual imagery and hardcore pornography can be the catalysts for tragedy.

Vulnerable children from broken homes who have had inadequate parenting are particularly at risk from violent videos. The greatest danger comes from the repetition of scenes which children repeatedly play back. Although it had become increasingly clear for many years that ongoing exposure to such videos leads to increasing callousness in some viewers, it was not until April 1994 that the government announced curbs to prevent children from watching them.

Despite all the evidence that custodial sentences do not reduce the crime rate, authority still relies heavily on imprisonment, usually in humiliating overcrowded and unsanitary conditions. Until very recently prison governors had been given even greater powers to discipline inmates. These included the right to hold the unruly in solitary confinement for up to fourteen days (instead of the then maximum of three) and to increase overall levels of austerity. Those who uphold the law, and those who break the law, have a moral responsibility to one another. Bigoted, inflexible and cruel parents have much in common with their violently angry children. Educating the former would lead to a decrease in the numbers of the latter.

Understanding the psychological parameters of crime not only helps to identify criminals, but also emphasises the importance of crime prevention through education. Crime is both a sickness and an attack on family life. While institutionalisation is necessary to protect the public from violent recidivists, and reparation by the criminal is important, preventative treatment – in the form of a clearer understanding of the role played by parents – should be obligatory.

These educational needs have never been formally adopted. But self-education is available to all. All that is required is a thoughtful curiosity. As adults reflect on the quality of the parenting that has led them to their lifestyle choices, the power of parenting will become increasingly apparent to all those embarking on it, other than the few whose disturbed personalities prevent them from recognising any social norms.

In many households, family meal times have fallen into desuetude and the kitchen is no longer the powerhouse of the home. The oven has been replaced by the microwave, home cooking by fast-food and takeaway, and mother by the TV. Simple steps can be taken to reverse this process. If given the choice between mother and television, children will, in fact, choose their mother. Will mothers, however, always choose the child? Such choices will only cease to be an option when the reason for the emotionally deprived's decision to steal the love that was denied them is more clearly understood.

3

Breaking and Entering

Buying love may be a psychosocial necessity.
But stealing it is rape.

If a woman has deprived her son of much of the emotional input to which he is entitled, he may see little wrong in helping himself at first to money from her bag, and later to assets belonging to other women (their sense of integrity and self-worth hidden within their vaginal 'purse').

Rape is an exercise in power by the essentially powerless caused by mothers who failed to empower their sons with the contentment, the security and ultimately the self-assurance due to them. Power gained as adults however may be used to humiliate and hurt. It is a power fuelled by the drive for sexual gratification, a power abused by men to avenge the real or apparent withholding of a mother's love. Men with cruel and abusive fathers may also sometimes steal what passes for 'love' from other men.

It is not only human beings who are the victims of man's acted-out rage. Other species are also prey to violent predators. Poachers ravage the world rhinoceros population for powdered rhinoceros horn, a supposed aphrodisiac. Their destructive activities in the interests of hyperarousal, like those of the rapist, feed into a violent and depredatory cycle. The environment needs protection from this sexually driven, although overtly financial, greed. More than one hundred and sixty years after the coming of the railways (an earlier, although ultimately creative, offender) the building of new roads through areas of natural beauty is still described by those concerned for the integrity of 'mother' earth, as the rape of the countryside.

That it is the drive for retaliation, as much as the sexual drive, which motivates rapists, is confirmed by the frequency with which

rape victims are humiliated by their insistence on exploitive procedures such as anal or oral intercourse. Although any woman may be
used as a stand-in for a mother, none will come closer to being the
real victim of a violent male's rage than a grandmother, a mother
no longer protected by the incest barrier. 'Granny-bashing' may not
seem to have an obvious sexual connotation, but a violent intrusion
into the privacy of a helpless woman, no matter what her age, is
nonetheless a form of rape.

A rapist may persuade himself that a woman enjoys the experience to which he submits her and that she secretly admires his
potency. Wanting to please her, as he would have once wanted to
please his mother, and hoping to make her love him, he may so
delude himself by his wishful thoughts that when caught he usually
claims that his victim not only consented to the act but welcomed it.
Rape and other forms of theft co-exist within a society where moral
and spiritual values take second place to greed and immediacy. An
abandoned woman left with a baby to bring up may not in fact have
been raped, but if sexual consent was obtained on the understanding that her partner's intentions were 'honourable', it is as if she had
been.

Women try to minimise the risk of rape but cannot always be on
their guard. In any event there is no defence against an armed man
under the influence of a hyperactive sex drive. There are usually few
warning signs, although a date rapist may sometimes be identified
by his persistent nagging and manipulative manner. It goes without
saying that being alone with a heavy drinker who has already signalled his intentions is dangerous and should be avoided.

In the long term, parents should be aware of the need to give
their children enough love so that they may transact it affectionately
with others later. In the shorter term, the outlook is poor. In 1992,
after an alcoholic New Year's Eve party, a young army officer found
himself in bed with his date for the evening. He wanted sex. She did
not. For attempting to have sex with her, he was sent to prison for
three years. In May 1994, on appeal, his sentence was reduced to two
years, while in 1995 a merciful (male) disciplinary tribunal decided
that his alcohol-induced 'indiscretion' was such that it would only
be necessary to suspend him from his regiment for a year.

Those who have not formally agreed to have sex with another (non-contractual intimacy), but have been coerced into doing so when either, or both, are under the influence of drugs or alcohol, are clearly the victims of an exploitive act. The lack of feeling implicit in the act may be contributed to by the tendency to teach very young children the facts of life before they are emotionally prepared for them. This may encourage a cold and mechanical approach to sex later. Affection cannot be taught at school, it can only be learned at home by small children with loving parents. But what if children are not at home? In 2004 the director of the Family Education Trust, Norman Wells, pointed out that government policy on the family 'has led to a crisis of identity among parents. On one hand they are held responsible for their children's behaviour at school and in the community, and on the other their role is being undermined by growing pressure to work outside the home'. He did not mention the role played by commercially greedy day nurseries. In August 2004 secret filming inside three day nurseries revealed women passing as carers who, far from helping infants to cope with the temporary absence of a loving mother, were not only indifferent to their needs but were actually bullying them.

Rape, an offence under the Sexual Offences Act, is defined as the loss of sexual control resulting in the forceful violation or ravishing of (usually) a woman either vaginally or anally. The crime of rape includes sex by all forms of improperly obtained consent whether by threats or false pretences, by the administration of drugs, sex with children or with the mentally disordered, or as an act of incest. Homosexual rape is also an indictable offence – the first case was tried in a British court in June 1995.

There is widespread revulsion against rape. In 2004 a man convicted of rape sixteen years earlier, on day release, and approaching the end of his sentence, bought a lottery ticket and won £7 million. The public's reaction was that the prize money should be distributed to his victims – confirmed by a legal ruling in 2008 that permitted his victims to pursue a belated case for damages against him. The reaction of the rapist is not known but had he acquired any insight into his childhood during his years in prison he might have acknowledged that since nothing had been given to him freely, having his lottery winnings withheld was no more than he could expect. Had he been left to decide what to do with his money and had chosen to contribute to a fund for the benefit of his victims, women might have been more confident of the effectiveness of prison rehabilitation.

Some judges in the past have taken the view that there are two forms of rape. In one an invariably violent stranger, often under the influence of drugs, threatens a woman (or a man) often with a knife, or a woman may be repeatedly raped by a gang. In the other a woman is raped by someone known to her who refused to take no for an answer. The judiciary is now persuaded that both forms of rape are equally reprehensible.

There is a third form of rape seldom recognised or acknowledged. It is neither criminal nor violent. It occurs in loving relationships where the woman's interest in sex is normal in theory but absent in practice. Her love for her partner is such that she accepts his sexual approaches but experiences it as rape. She does not verbalise her problem with him but uses body language instead.

> Cleo, brought up to be seen but not heard, was one of two daughters of a bullying father whose sole interest was running a small farm that had been in the family for generations. His insensitivity to his daughter's feelings took the form of ignoring her obvious talents. She excelled at ballet and music. She did not discuss this with him because she knew he was not interested in them.
>
> Cleo eventually found her soulmate. Gareth was a lawyer and articulate and friendly. She chose him because he was unlike her father. She loved him because he listened to her. Within a year their first child was born. Cleo was horrified when she began to see in Gareth, now a father of their child, some of the character traits she associated with her own father. Using sexual body language she 'explained' her predicament to him. She permitted penetrative sex but only with her back turned. She would squeeze Gareth's thigh between her legs. Putting pressure on his thigh and penis was uncomfortable because it prevented him from moving. Sex was not enjoyable. By turning her back on Gareth, by denying him pleasure and controlling sexual activity by holding his penis in a castrating

grip, Cleo had found a way of punishing him because he had come to remind her of her father.

While Cleo was growing up the law took the view that there was a binding contract for a wife to provide sex when her husband wanted it. She believed it was her duty to satisfy Gareth's sexual needs. More recently marital rape has been deemed a crime. Many men, who in the past have insisted on 'their rights,' have failed to recognise the cold shoulder (the cold vagina).

Cleo did not realise she had right on her side. She could have verbalised her hostility to Gareth when he became a father and with help resolved the problem. In a different setting she might also (perhaps with the help of an understanding mother) have chosen to verbalise her feelings to her father as a child. She would not then have needed to scapegoat another father for her own father's shortcomings.

Georgina, a thirty year-old married woman, was eighteen when she met and fell in love with Emrys. She had not expected a happy outcome from an abusive childhood. Her mother had died when she was thirteen and her bereaved father had gradually come to experience his daughter as her mother's replacement. She loved her father and she was sixteen before she felt strong enough to break the sexual bond he had imposed upon her.

She and Emrys were sexually active for three years until their daughter was born but soon afterwards her sexual responses began to fade. She attributed her lack of libido to childbirth rather than to her father's legacy. Georgina, like Cleo, struggled to accept her husband's advances but as time passed her sexual aversion to him became total.

In therapy she described her loving husband's sexual approaches as like that of a rapist. Childbirth had indeed caused her loss of libido not because it had introduced a baby into their relationship but because it had changed her husband into a father. Like Gareth the image of her abusive father had become superimposed over her husband and sexual contact between them was once again experienced by her as incestuous; distasteful and forbidden.

An understanding of their problem saved their marriage and a cognitive behavioural approach restored their sex life.

Sex with a consenting, but underage, child also qualifies as rape. In 1996 an eighteen-year-old Turkish male married an English girl of thirteen in a religious ceremony in Turkey. In her absence she was made a ward of court in England, while in Turkey her husband was arrested and charged with raping her.

The judiciary seldom has difficulty in invoking the law when forcible sexual intercourse was committed by a stranger, although it has been known to express doubt when the rape has been perpetrated by a person known to the victim. The circumstances of rape continues to cause controversy, and the view that rape is shameful and degrading not just to the victim but also to the perpetrator is widely held. In 2007 in Saudi Arabia, a country in which women have no rights, a young woman and a male friend were gang raped. The woman was sentenced to 200 lashes by a male judge for being in the company of a male in the absence of a chaperone. Following worldwide repugnance the Saudi authorities withdrew the penalty.

This was not the case however at Marion County Court, Indianapolis, in February 1992. World-heavyweight boxing champion, Mike Tyson, found himself before Judge Patricia Gifford charged with raping Desirée Washington (a participant in the 1991 Miss Black America contest), whom he had met some hours earlier. Desirée had agreed to go to Tyson's hotel room, but claimed that she had refused sex with him. Tyson said she was a willing sex partner. It was her word against his. The judge believed Desirée's version of the events and Tyson went to prison, serving three years of an eight-year sentence. Tyson resumed his boxing career and in 1996 successfully defended his world title. His offence was soon forgotten by the mostly male spectators who found a convenient outlet in boxing for their own suppressed violence. Thirteen months after his release however, he was falsely accused of making sexual advances to a woman in a night club. She had made the mistake of thinking that any male seeking to make a conquest in the ring is equally determined to make a (sexual) conquest out of it. In a brief moment of role reversal, Mike Tyson felt what it must have been like to have been Desirée Washington. By 2004 Mike Tyson was not only bankrupt owing $27 million, but was defeated in a world title fight by a little known newcomer. In his twenty-year boxing career during which time he had earned $300 million, Mike Tyson had fought for love, been sent to prison for stealing love, and had invited love from his wife and children by spending vast sums of money on gifts for them. His parents had they so wished, could have loved him for nothing.

Lesser degrees of sexual intrusion are commonplace, at work, in the street, and in marriage. Few women raise serious objections to the unsolicited and unwanted sexual comments made by men, often in public, to unaccompanied women. If they do complain, it may be a considerable time before anything is done to remedy the situation. In November 1993 a woman fire-fighter (there is still no female descriptive term) was awarded £10,000 in damages, after claiming sexual harassment at work. She complained that she had been thrown on to the bonnet of a Land Rover and that a fireman had stood between her legs and simulated sexual intercourse with her. On another occasion another fireman had forced her head down on to his lap. A £10,000 fine seems a small penalty to pay for a gross violation of a woman's rights. The Fire Service has always been male dominated, for fairly obvious phallic reasons, and at the time clearly resented the intrusion of women. It was only after this complaint that new guidelines were introduced to avoid a recurrence of such incidents.

In other parts of the world, the problem of unwanted sexual intrusion is also beginning to be addressed. In Japan's labour ministry the concept of sexual harassment, hitherto unrecognised, has at least been defined. It is said to constitute 'unpleasant speech or conduct with sexual references that creates a difficult work environment'. A survey conducted in 1991 in Japan, revealed that forty-four per cent of male office workers did not believe that asking a woman colleague the colour of her underwear constituted a sexual intrusion. A further survey fifteen years later showed that twenty-six per cent of working women in Tokyo had suffered 'at least one unpleasant sexual experience at work in the past two years'.

The tendency of women to laugh off the wolf whistle does little for the rights of the individual, either male or female. The problem of the predatory male and the helpless female is becoming increasingly confronted. The piercing sound of the rape whistle, and the mobile phone for the late-night breakdown and subsequent break-in, are welcome additions to a woman's anti-harassment armamentarium.

Homosexual rape, always a possibility in same sex institutions such as prisons, has occasionally been reported in urban areas and gang rape seems to be just one more drug-related statistic in a society where little thought has been given to the future of a child who has grown up without the benefit of motherly love. It is ironic that the rapist's victim may also be a mother of other neglected children, making rape a once removed, victim-provoked crime. Revenge may be sweet but when victims scapegoat innocent others, the fallout of abusive parenting is perpetuated.

4

Payback Time

An eye for an eye will make the whole world blind.

Mahatma Gandhi

Once started, cycles of abuse and retribution take on a life of their own. Feelings of humiliation, the legacy of childhood, are not easily contained and many victims offload their feelings on to other victims, whom they seek out or create for that purpose, thereby themselves becoming persecutors. If their timidity does not allow for this, victims may harm themselves. Victims are attracted to persecutors and may become emotionally involved with them. They have convinced themselves that persecutors need them and they need persecutors. They have not chosen any of this. Abusive parents have chosen it for them.

Members of groups, ethnic or religious, are frequently victimised, the stronger and more numerous discriminating against the weaker and the fewer. Underdogs are exploited because they are weak; Blacks, Asians, Jews and gays because they are different; children because their parents have not tuned into their needs and women because of their gender. Racism, sexuality, poverty and childcare are now beginning to be addressed but in 1928 when Sigmund Freud asked Princess Marie Buonaparte, one of his pupils – herself a psychoanalyst and the wife of Prince George of Greece – 'What do women want?' he believed that they were mainly preoccupied with penis envy. He did not enquire about the needs of Jews or gays or gypsies, other victims of prejudice – only women. Why was he sharing with Marie Buonaparte his frustrations about his failure to come to grips with the sexuality of women? Did he believe that the sexual approaches of men, perhaps including his own, were not only provoked by women – a not uncommon feature of male grandiosity

– but were actually welcomed by them? Freud's lack of hands-on parenting, common in the nineteenth century, may have bothered him but it did not lead to his stealing love (although he is thought to have had an affair with his wife's sister) but to research into the sexuality of children, essentially into a boy's fear of losing his penis (castration anxiety) and a girl's wish for one (penis envy).

In nineteenth-century England a woman might have allowed a prospective husband a glimpse of an ankle. Today when minuscule skirts, skin-tight sweaters, bare midriffs, visible thongs and other erotic signals expose far more of the female body, men's testosterone-driven and hair-trigger sexual responses should logically be more easily stimulated, and Freud's enquiry of Marie Buonaparte more easily answered. It is not. Frequent exposure to the same sexual stimulus will eventually lead to apathy and may account for the general diminution of erotic intensity in marriage compared with the passion (albeit often short-lived) of an affair. The glimpse of the ankle – like the brief fling – depends less on what it might develop into but more on what it is. Men can hardly be blamed because the goal posts have moved; neither should women need to excuse themselves for following the dictates of fashion. As for women, a full enquiry into their needs and in particular their interaction with their children when their needs are not met is long overdue.

Increasing numbers of young men and women, having had their need for loving approval enhanced not by erotic signals but by the too frequent absences of parents, are destined to choose a lifestyle seeking, and sometimes stealing, the admiration on which they missed out. Some unloved children run away, a re-enactment of feeling more 'at home' away from home, in the street.

An ideal childhood is yet to exist and aberrant parenting will continue to be hedged about by regulation as penalty takes over from enquiry. The Sexual Discrimination Act, the industrial tribunal, the veil, and instruction in moral issues may protect an adult female from sexual harassment, but they cannot protect her from abused children when they are in payback mode.

Henrietta, a forty-year-old attractive, unmarried woman, often reflected on her deprived childhood in a well-to-do home. Her mother loved her but her father frequently physically abused her, although never sexually. She grew up to believe that he preferred her younger sister, and that had she been physically more pleasing, he would have been more loving towards her. Henrietta hates what she thinks of as her unattractive body, abuses it by dieting and binge-ing, sometimes deliberately cuts parts of it and is unable to accept herself as she is. Because of her upbringing she sets up situations which make it hard for men to admire her. She does not want to have children because she knows that if she were to become a parent she might treat them as her father had treated her. A sad and unfortu-nate victim of her childhood, Henrietta rebuffs and scapegoats all men, because one man – her father – was indifferent to her needs. If Henrietta does marry, it will probably be when it is too late for her to conceive – a high price to pay to prevent a similar dysfunctional pattern of behaviour repeating itself.

Victims of abuse such as Henrietta are right to be angry. Some regress, as adolescents, into early childhood and use body language to express their feelings. Bingeing on food, the symbol of maternal attention, leads others to adopt a pattern of behaviour to which they soon become addicted. Food bingeing encapsulates both a need for, and hostility to the mother since bingeing is usually followed by vomiting. Retaliating against mothers by metaphorically throwing back feeds in the face of the mother who fed them, is not only the ultimate in payback but also reflects the extra time their mother is forced to spend with them, cleaning up after them in infancy.

Helen, a twenty-five-year-old married mother, would visit her mother most weekends accompanied by her four year-old son. As a child Helen had frequently been in conflict with her neglectful mother. She was seldom satisfied with her input and became a fussy eater as a teenager. The doting grandmother, delighted to see her grandchild on such a regular basis, had a cupboard full of his favour-ite toys. On his arrival he would go straight to the cupboard and pull out the neatly stacked bricks and little cars with which he would then play until it was time to go home. Helen had never binged nor vomited but she soon discovered that there were other more subtle ways of showing her hostility to her mother. She never tidied up after her visit with her child however much of a mess he made. She had at last found a way of attacking her now elderly mother by switching roles with her young son. Her mother's regular comment to Helen's grandfather each week after her daughter had left was 'Why does she always trash our home?' Neither realised that Helen's unconscious was telling her that her mother had trashed her childhood and that now it was payback time.

Victims of deprived childhoods may seek illusory and potentially damaging 'nurturing' from other sources, such as drugs, sex, alcohol or from the compulsive acquisition of money. Some women, abused by their fathers, may attempt to deny their femininity by starving themselves into a non-menstruating pre-pubertal childlike state so that men will find them unattractive.

Growing up does not guarantee escape from the confines of a disturbed upbringing. Only adequate love ensures the opening up of the circular mother/child and later father/child commitment. The unloved continue to fear enclosure – whether emotional or physical and remain attached to the family home, patiently but pointlessly, waiting for the security they missed out on to manifest itself.

Unselfish and unconditional love is hard to come by, particularly for those who grow up in broken homes. When children are given only conditional love by their remaining parent – who may in addition depend on them to make up for what they themselves have lost – they will rightly feel exploited. It is never too late for the adult victims of such an upbringing to learn how to convert the anger which they were obliged to suppress in childhood into more creative channels. But if appropriate ways of dealing with this anger are not found, it becomes murderous in its intensity. Victims without a conscience are dangerous and may penalise others. Victims with a conscience usually penalise themselves.

Parents whose authoritarian and demanding attitudes have contributed to these problems are only rarely confronted by their children who will remain afraid of them until they eventually come to realise that their now elderly parents bear little relationship to yesterday's autocrats. Many parents are only too willing to believe that economic factors, over which they have no control, are to blame for the antisocial and abusive behaviour of their children. It is not lack of financial security but emotional security that causes children to suffer from, and react to, their childhood.

An absentee mother may well have wished to have spent more time with her child. A sole breadwinner would not have been able to. Paid maternity leave has gone some way towards solving the problem. The paid surrogate has not. Child-rearing cannot be considered as a career choice by women because it is not rewarded by adequate state benefits. The problems therefore that arise from an emotionally deprived childhood will never be completely addressed until child-rearing is accepted as a paid career choice. Women have a right to be 'as men' in the workplace but not at the expense of being 'as women' in the home. A woman may become an airline pilot but a man will never breastfeed a baby.

The children of women who do not work may also feel neglected if they are left for too long with care-givers if their parents take holidays without them. Infants will experience this separation as the withholding of love. If children less than a year old do not see their mother for more than two weeks, they may not recognise her when she reappears. Their expectations of abandonment will affect their adult relationships.

Payback time (from emotional neglect to sexual abuse) is passed on through the generations. Twenty-one per cent of male college students who were themselves abused have admitted that they feel sexually attracted to young children. Five per cent said that they would actually abuse children if they thought that they could get away with it. About thirty-five per cent of all child abusers are teenagers, and childcare professionals emphasise the importance of helping them empathise with their victims. They might then see them not merely as scapegoats, but as fellow sufferers.

Despite the increasing number of studies showing that children who received low levels of maternal support have understandably high levels of behavioural problems, it is only now being recognised that encouraging parenting classes is more likely to prevent retaliatory antisocial behaviour than penalising those who offend with longer prison sentences. Home Secretaries continue to insist on harsh sentences as a means of reducing the increasing incidence of crime. Out of touch with the ongoing cycle of intergenerational revenge they may choose to ignore those who believe that custodial sentences should be confined to the dangerous, the recidivist and the criminally insane. A prison sentence, given not to protect society but to act as a deterrent, is acknowledged to be ineffective and no more so than for those who scapegoat others for what their parents did to them. Prison is a school where the victims of a criminal upbringing learn only how to become better criminals.

The number of criminals in prison in 2007 in Britain – more than 80,000 – is more than double the figure for 1991. The number of prospective parents attending parenting classes, in the unlikely event that any exist in their area, is virtually nil despite evidence that the cognitive therapy on offer is recognised as extremely helpful by the few who have had experience of it. One question seldom addressed, is whether society's victims unconsciously set up situations in which they might be thought to be colluding with the criminal, on the grounds that injustice is what they must expect from life.

It was once suggested by a Law Lord that car owners should be fined for leaving their car doors unlocked. A sad commentary on changing times. It was not so long ago that it was safe and indeed neighbourly to leave front doors unlocked. We can protect our property, we can lock up our daughters, or we could stay at home and look after them! Should we take the law into our own hands? Liberal attitudes towards individual responsibility for crime prevention may seem praiseworthy, but defending oneself too vigorously may lead to a charge of grievous bodily harm being brought against the criminal's victim. In a survey carried out on behalf of the BBC's *Today* programme in January 2004, 'liberal' opinion (presumably those who stay at home and read the newspapers or listen to the radio) was shocked by the fact that a majority of those taking part in the survey voted in favour of householders using violence towards anyone found breaking into their homes.

In a modern democracy there is no case to be made for making 'the punishment fit the crime' and certainly not a generation after it. In the recent past some seemed happy enough to tolerate the lashing with a bamboo cane of an American student in Borneo caught van-dalising cars. In Saudi Arabia, cutting off the hand of those convicted of stealing, and both hands from those who re-offend, makes repeti-tion of theft impossible and accounts for a low crime rate second to none. No Western country would want to emulate such an example.

The establishment (parents) has a vested interest in blaming the rising crime rate not on emotional deprivation but on intoxication induced by the use of mind-altering drugs. It is however less likely that a child from a psychologically healthy, loving and supportive family, however poor, will in adult life, seek the illusory comfort provided by chemicals, or even worse the equally illusory comfort of 'sticking his knife into' the child of another mother.

5

Bullying and Abuse

Before you can say knife.

Child abuse begins within the confines of early infancy. The first confinement, within the womb, is closely followed by a second in the encircling arms of a mother. If the embrace is warm and fulfils the child's emotional needs he will be off to a good start. If it fails to result in the contentment and security to which he is entitled, and is later followed by negative interactions with his father, the scene will be set for the unloading on to others of the ongoing resentment at having been cheated of his birthright. All subsequent enclosures – either emotional or concrete such as school, marriage, the armed services, the workplace, lifts, travel and even the confines of pregnancy, of time and of religious ritual – will not only remind him of his unhappy childhood but will in some cases lead to phobic avoidance of these enclosures or to the abuse of others. In 2004, the children's charity Childline reported that the number of victims of bullying in schools had risen by a record forty-two per cent. Esther Rantzen, the charity's onetime chair thought that reality TV in some instances endorsed bullying, notably *Hell's Kitchen* and other similar programmes in which the chef verbally abuses other chefs. Could his passionate interest in cooking and his apparent conviction that he is a far better feeder than any mother, possibly reflect his experiences with his own mother? Childline answers 2,300 calls a day on its helpline and recommends that concerned parents should be taught how to recognise bullying in their children and also how to help a bullied child. But as yet it has not been possible to teach parents what steps to take to avoid their children passing on their experiences of an abusive childhood to others. A parentline on which parents could call for help in giving up abusing their children is needed.

Away from the powerhouse of the kitchen, the domain of the mother, and the enclosed environment of the boarding school, the domain of the matron, more spectacular forms of abuse take place in which younger boys are exposed to extreme cruelty. The unwitting demeanour and expectation of an abused child will invite the attentions of a bully, usually an older boy, who was probably a victim himself and who will seize any opportunity to seek revenge. Boarding schools are suited only to children who have been loved sufficiently by their parents to allow them to be temporarily separated from them. At the age of seven, few children will feel sufficiently secure to cope with being sent to an institution in which, surrounded by sometimes violent strangers, they may be permanently psychologically damaged. An insufficiently loved or worse, abused new boy will be the target of an older child's previously unexpressed misery. The bully will seek relief for his own unhappiness, by downloading the constipated waste products of parental neglect, on to an equally helpless child.

It is no coincidence that school bullying often takes place in the lavatory. Such a scene is graphically depicted in the film *If* (Lindsay Anderson, 1968), a portrayal of life at a boy's public school. 'I've taken just about enough shit from you as I can stand.' The victim's head is then pushed into the lavatory bowl which is flushed in a symbolic washing away of the accumulated rubbish of a cruel upbringing. Bullying at school, once thought of as gender specific, has now spread to girls. In 2004 forty girls were caught on CCTV at a school in Dorset and temporally suspended for physically attacking another girl, ostensibly in a row over a boy.

Although there can be no excuse for the attitude of teachers who allow small boys to be persecuted by older boys on the grounds that 'boys will be boys,' active abuse carried out by teachers themselves is even more inexcusable. Disturbed children in care, and confined to local authority homes, are particularly vulnerable. In common with the weak and disadvantaged everywhere, they inevitably invite the attentions of sadists. Nowhere was this more evident than in the behaviour of American Military Police in the Abu Ghraib confinement facility in Baghdad between October and December 2003. Iraqi prisoners, many suspected of terrorist activities, were sadistically abused to encourage them to talk of their activities. American military personnel, some of them women, were ordered by one US government agency or another to humiliate prisoners, often sexually and in some cases to threaten them with death. Some soldiers took trophy photographs which were later reproduced in the newspapers. Donald Rumsfeld, the US Secretary of Defence and President George W. Bush both apologised for what they described as 'totally unacceptable and un-American behaviour' and promised that the perpetrators would face a court martial.

Prisoners of war, better described as victims of war, are rendered helpless by their circumstances and apologists claim that in such circumstances, abuses, although unacceptable, are not uncommon. Those ordered onto the battlefield, it is suggested, must accept its horrors. But it is not only on the battlefield that abuses in the Armed Services occur. Abuse may also occur in peacetime. British newspaper headlines (September 1987): 'Army bullies jailed for torment of new recruits', and 'Ex-soldiers gaoled for degrading rites', bear a very close resemblance to similar bullying at school. Two former soldiers had admitted to ordering recruits 'to get on top of one another and have sex', and forcing them to sit in a cold bath containing urine and human excrement. They were also put into a cupboard in which CS gas was released. The defence lawyers at the court martial said that the two accused had themselves been through initiation ceremonies and believed that 'there was no harm in it'.

Another institution, as emotionally controlling as other more physical enclosures, is that of fundamentalist religion. Some of the practices imposed by priests in the name of procreational sex are only now beginning to be condemned. Female circumcision (female genital mutilation) is inflicted on about eighty million pre-pubertal girls throughout the world each year. The aim of this operation is to ensure premarital virginity. It also aims to discourage sexual promiscuity, by making casual sex impossible and sexual pleasure virtually unattainable.

Children do not expect to face horrors when in the care of professionals supposedly concerned entirely with their well-being and in *loco parentis*. Perhaps they should. The principal of a community home in the north of England admitted to twelve charges of sexual and indecent assault on nine boys under his care between 1973 and 1980. The boys had complained to the authorities over the seven-year period, but they were not believed. In 1990 one young victim cut his wrists in despair, but it was not until 1992 – following a belated police enquiry – that the principal, having confessed to the sexual offences, was finally arrested and jailed. Although it is the duty of the social services to vet the conduct of all males in positions of responsibility in institutions under their jurisdiction, this duty is often carried out inadequately. In another case in 1997 the chief executive of a top security mental hospital and eight nurses were suspended after it had been alleged that a paedophile ring was being run from the Personality Disorder Unit.

Children may also be exposed in less obvious ways to abuse from sadistic adults. Videos, available to children, overtly celebrate the abuse of women. They also abuse the sensitivities of the underage viewer. While these videos carry an '18' certificate, this does not deter ten- to fourteen-year-olds from acquiring them. Animated sex can be more grotesquely violent and offensive than straightforward pornography. On more than one occasion in the recent past animated cartoons have been in the top ten. Boasting the latest technology, they depict rape of underage girls, oral sex and masturbation.

Abuse of children is often obscured by the behaviour of members of bizarre sects masquerading as purveyors of family love. During the 1990s there were up to 500 religious cults in Britain alone. Indoctrination of the vulnerable is a feature of them all. In Argentina in September 1993, 140 children were taken into custodial care and eighteen adults were charged with sexual abuse of children, enslavement, concealment of minors, and racial and religious discrimination. Physical and psychological examination of the children demonstrated that the boys had anal injuries and the girls torn hymens. The Children of God – a 'sex-for-salvation' cult taking refuge behind quasi-religious beliefs – claimed that the arrests subjected them to religious persecution. In fact the only religious belief that the cult continued to insist upon was that God advocated free love and that sex was the avenue to salvation.

The fictional community in William Golding's *Lord of the Flies* illustrates how small boys re-enact the worst of the parent/child experience. A plane load of children survive a forced landing on a deserted island. Their behaviour, until their rescue, not only reflects their early childhood experiences, but previews the prejudices, savagery, and violence (in addition to the many positive attributes) which will inform their adult lives.

By 2004 gun crime had risen to record levels, despite the introduction of tough new prison sentences, closely followed by knife crime in 2008. There was a clear link between such offences and the increasing use of crack cocaine and alcohol. Harsher sentences were recommended as a remedy for violence with occasional mention of involving the community, including parents to help in combating it. Good as far as it goes. But since neglected babies become angry adults and 'abusive parents beget abusive children' who seek comfort later from drugs, asking parents to help once the damage is done will always be too late.

A vulnerable child will, at some stage in his life, act out his reaction to his abusive upbringing. Sexual crime has its roots in the sexual abuse of the perpetrators. This accounts for the lengths to which abusive parents will go in shutting their eyes to the sins of their children for whom they are responsible. There are many who believe that it is television not they who have brought violence into the home and made it acceptable (mainly to boys).

The same parents also take a view about their children's toys. In both the UK and the US, toy shops have reported a dramatic fall in the sale of guns – and some even refuse to stock them. Toy guns, like violent videos, certainly feed into and reinforce violence. But a child's behaviour can only be reinforced if his environment was violent in the first place. A loved and secure child will not be turned into an antisocial misfit either by watching videos or by playing with toy soldiers and guns.

Abuse in the workplace re-enacts the hostility felt by men for cold and distant mothers, when under cover of flattery and flirtatiousness, they scapegoat women. Many women, still either ignore sexual harassment, or treat it, and the men responsible for it, with contempt. A few feel humiliated and degraded. Should the sexual harassment persist, women may refer the matter to an industrial tribunal which has the authority to invoke the Sex Discrimination Act 1975 (amended in 2003) and the penalties contained within it.

A claustrophobic marriage may encourage someone who has been exploited as a child to reject his partner. The marriage vows, and the earlier broken (albeit unspoken) vows of mother to child, become linked in the mind of the adult. An open-ended cohabitation may often be the best choice for an unloved and exploited child.

Bad parenting has much to answer for. But only its more gross forms are easily recognised. Parents abuse their power when they unite in opposition to the needs of a child who can then abandon all hope of fair treatment. When the persecutors are two adults and the defendant a small child with no one to speak for him, the outcome will not be in doubt. In the courts the case for the defendant is always presented by an advocate, but in the home, parents who collude in accusing their children of misdemeanours, deny them this basic right. When faced with negative behaviour, admonishments dredged from their own past – often beginning with the word 'don't' – automatically surface.

The less a parent has been loved by his own parents, the more love will he expect from his children. To ensure that he receives this 'love', he may threaten the withholding of approval and a privilege if a child does not live up to his demands for it. A child brought up to believe that his parents will never be entirely pleased with him, will eventually come to the conclusion that he is essentially unworthy. The seeds of self-esteem are sown at home. Those who grow up without a sense of self-worth are obliged as adults to seek inappropriate compensations.

A robust child may resist parental manipulation. Parents may try to assert their authority by physical means. A child who is physically attacked will feel humiliated. It is an unequal contest. 'A good smack never did me any harm' is a comment heard not only from the lips of those who deride liberal child-rearing practices. Former Prime Minister Tony Blair admitted that he smacked his three children when they were little but had to admit that he felt 'some remorse'.

Children, like adults, experience negative as well as positive feelings. It would be unreasonable of parents always to expect 'polite' responses from them. Negative feelings where appropriate, are normal. If these feelings are suppressed they will surface later when they will have ceased to be acceptable. Envy of the breast – which the child believes contains love withheld from him and which results in a momentary but nonetheless passionate rage directed at the mother – is normal. Jealousy – when this love is given to a sibling – is normal. Anger, when a child is frustrated or kept waiting is normal. Occasional 'violent' attacks on younger brothers and sisters, who have displaced them, are normal. 'Greedy' demands for food or attention are normal.

But many parents have had to comply with parental demands themselves and see no reason why their children should not do the same. When a father expects his daughter to please him by complying with his wishes, the first step towards abuse will have been taken. The second step is taken when he looks to her to comply with his sexual wishes. This step is irreversible. It could be prevented by a mother with courage enough to protect her child from the demands of her probably psychopathic, and sometimes violent, partner. Some mothers, however, collude with their partner's exploitive behaviour, either because they are relieved to have the unwelcome attentions of an aggressive or demanding bully diverted from them or because they are themselves psychologically damaged.

A young girl may at first accept sexual contact with her father as normal. Other siblings may even be jealous of the attention she is getting, and she herself may welcome the extra 'love' she receives. As puberty approaches she will come to recognise that she is being abused, but by then she will usually be too ashamed to ask for help.

The issue of modesty is seldom addressed, other than by the mothers of pubescent children and by those whose religious beliefs insist on women wearing clothing that covers every aspect of their femininity. The rights of women continue to be ignored in the interpretations and practices of some of the major religions, and the rights of children continue to be ignored by abusive parents. In a democratic family, men, women and children have equal rights. In an autocratic family only adult males have rights, the family unit is totalitarian, and the father a dictator. The children grow up to be anxious in all 'non-escape' situations. Making love would seem to be far less damaging a remedy for those concerned with the absence of their rights (with some social reservations), than making war.

6

Sexual Deviation

Sex is totally ludicrous to everybody except the participants.

Alan Plater

The intensely pleasurable feelings characteristic of adult sex is almost certainly a successor to the highly charged emotional exchanges between a mother and her infant. Both are more or less oblivious to everything other than the tasks in hand ranging from breastfeeding to nappy-changing. When in adult life these emotional exchanges are overemphasised because of their insufficient fulfilment during infancy it will usually be more in the interests of recreational than procreational sex. The child's sexual attachment to the mother which Freud believed would come to an end at about the age of four will remain, encouraging them as adults to choose partners with caring 'motherly' qualities.

Re-enacting nursery interactions, years later, with another partner, and being lost in the fantasies that reinforce them, is regarded as bizarre by non-participants, and deviant or perverse by religions which emphasise sex primarily as a procreational activity.

While breastfeeding is taking place a male infant may experience a reflex erection, and a female infant, vaginal contraction. Sucking and kissing, looking and exhibiting, stroking, squeezing and genital fondling are major features of an infant's love affair with his mother. If these activities take place in a loving and accepting setting, from puberty onwards the child will be prepared for adult genital sexuality. If mothers fail to fulfil their children's primitive presexual needs they will look to satisfy them in similarly intimate situations later. Mothers respond to their infant's needs mainly by feeding. Intimacy, security, emotional gratification, instant availability, dependency and commitment however also demand fulfilment. These needs are communicated by the infant to the mother using body language and are responded to by the mother. When aspects of their fulfilment are denied they will be sought later. They may then be described by some as deviant or perverse.

While adult sexual activity is shaped by a child's early experiences with the mother, later interactions between father and son, and between father and daughter (abusive or loving) may influence not only partner choice in adult life but will also play a role both in sexual preferences and, in those who already have a genetic and/or hormonal predisposition, in sexual orientation.

Variations in essentially unchanging preferences during sexual activity, if requested by one partner or the other, may be considered contentious by those who have been exposed to other variables in infancy and will usually be declined. If they are accepted in the interests of harmony they will not necessarily be experienced as agreeable. The risk to an established partnership is that the individual whose needs are not satisfied is left with unfulfilled expectations which demand to be filled and is at risk for seeking gratification elsewhere. Falling in love with another is an overwhelming sensation difficult to resist. Victims are drawn back to the time when all physical needs were expected to be gratified by a permanent and available attendant. Falling in love may be only temporary and is frequently repeated. It cannot always be relied upon as a guarantee of lifetime happiness.

> Ben, a fifty-year-old father of four boys, had been reasonably happily married for twenty years when he was struck by a *coup de foudre* so intense that he became incapable of reasoned thought. He described his escape from his marriage as a sense of freedom akin to how he felt when occasionally, late at night, perhaps in a symbolic return to the womb, he would swim naked in the sea. He re-experienced this feeling of freedom when on another occasion he wore a dress belonging to his girlfriend. He felt so at one with her that actually being in her clothes allowed him the illusion that he was her, a closeness that he might have expected to experience in infancy with his mother.

The sensations involved in deviant sex are entirely appropriate to the primitive needs of the infant. When reasoned thought begins to develop, these sensations will evolve into love and affection. An urgent drive to fulfil erotic needs, at the expense of affection in adult life, suggests that the early gratifications of infancy were either insufficient for the infant's needs or that affectionate interaction with carers failed to develop.

Infants and mothers have a tentative relationship to begin with but within days mother and baby will be learning to trust one another. Not all mothers and babies bond immediately but they soon realise that they love one another. Even love at first sight has to be worked upon. Mouth-breast 'intercourse' is initiated by the infant, and most mothers respond immediately to it. The bonding process is established and later becomes the basis for a similar bond with an adult partner. These intimate moments are as gratifying to the male infant as intercourse with a female will be later, with the penis replacing the breast and the vagina the mouth. For female infants, the breast remains the breast with 'bosom' friendships and the milk (of human kindness) representing adult caring attachments. The gradual coming together of erotic and affectionate feelings are essential components of mature adult love. Since the appetite for food is as unremitting a hunger as is later the appetite for sex, its gratification, at least in infancy, cannot be delayed. In adult life it may be put on hold in the interests of family, friendship, a loving concern for the health and well-being of the other, or the demands of religious celibacy.

Men and women may scapegoat one another for an insensitive parent's failure to fulfil their earlier emotional needs. Those who were loved as children will share this love in adult life, while those who were hurt or humiliated, are likely to hurt or humiliate others. Because of what they have been brought up to expect, some adults unwittingly set up situations in which their partners treat them as their parents did. When the primary aim of sexual activity is self-gratification the needs of a partner are seldom considered. When self-gratification sex excludes penetrative sex entirely, the activity is referred to as a paraphilia.

Most paraphilias, particularly the dangerous ones, occur in the male. Some males, particularly those who abuse children may never be 'cured' and when released from custodial sentences need indefinite monitoring by the police and social services. Dangerous paraphilias include sado-masochistic practices, erotic strangulation-suicide, lust murder and heterosexual, homosexual, or paedophilic rape. These paraphilias, considered by some to have genetic components, require particularly sensitive parenting. This is difficult to achieve since such paraphilias are almost impossible to recognise before puberty.

Other paraphilias such as clothes fetishism, preference for partial – as opposed to total – nudity, and sexual stimulation using visual erotic imagery, are not only harmless but throw light on early child/ parent interaction. The fantasised content may often be a reflection of child/parent hostility. The use of fantasy during masturbation or with a partner is normal. Most men and women use fantasy to enhance erotic response but many are too embarrassed to talk about it. The fantasised partner, originally the mother, is often replaced in adult life by another carer. A nurse is the quintessential carer for a male and a doctor may play the same role for a female.

Ed, a fifty-two-year-old surgeon, who loved his wife and children dearly and had no intention of leaving them, had a sexual fantasy that illuminates the importance of the mother/baby relationship. He was too embarrassed to discuss his fantasy with his wife but was compelled to act it out with his scrub nurse (with whom he was having an affair) in the clinic in which they worked. He would lie on his back on the operating table with his knees drawn up in the nappy changing position. The nurse, dressed in her scrubs, would stand at the foot of the table facing him. He would be so aroused by the position he was in and by the presence of the nurse that ejaculation would occur often without any physical contact between them. The fact that he had never forgotten an activity which had so impressed him over half a century earlier, gradually helped him come to terms with other reactions to his early life.

Those who practise non-dangerous sadism, anal intercourse, bondage or rarely, the contemptuous and humiliating soiling of women with urine or faeces, are usually men who have an antipathy to women. Men who are afraid of women are more sexually aroused when the vagina is partially obscured by a fetish such as transparent underwear. A fetish whether clothing, looking, telephoning or emailing often takes on a life of its own and may become an alternative sexual object. Fetishistic objects are sometimes so eroticised that silk, rubber or hair, stalking, uninvited touching, looking, or being looked at, may make an actual partner redundant.

Fetishism in women focuses on hair and clothing and is used to accentuate sexuality, rather than hide it. Women who signal sexuality in this way may be challenging anxious men who tend to keep women at a distance.

An out-of-reach mother in childhood leads to arm's length sex in adult life. Exhibitionism, voyeurism, and remote communication such as repeated telephone calls or text messages (obscene or simply for reassurance) make arousal possible for those for whom the bonding and closeness of a loving mother was unavailable. Playful beating, positions during intercourse and bondage also reflect memories of early overemphasised mother/child physical interactions.

Certain coital positions may be reminders of a dominant or controlling parent. A woman who habitually turns her back on her partner during penetration may be using him as a scapegoat for a distant or absent father. A man, who prefers a woman's back to be turned to him during sexual activity, may be recalling his earlier relationship with his mother, from whom he learned that love and rejection were inseparable. Some men prefer women to be in the superior position, recalling the dominant mother who both loved and controlled them. Others retaliate against controlling mothers by insisting on non-penetrative sex, thereby controlling their partner's instinctual reproductive needs and their pleasurable responses.

A woman will take charge when she insists on sexual intercourse at the time of ovulation in order to become pregnant. Some men may find such demands difficult to meet, not only because of the absence of spontaneity, but because 'a woman in the driving seat' is unacceptable and may lead to transient impotence. A sexually fragile man may feel that his partner has robbed him of his potency. Others, who require a good deal of recreational sexual activity before vaginal penetration, become resentful when, anxious to become pregnant, their partners do not want to 'waste time' in foreplay.

Although most women recognise that playing the dominant role in the interests of fertility may make some men uneasy, their pro-creative needs are so insistent that they cannot easily be delayed, particularly when there is peer group pressure to become pregnant, or when the menopause approaches.

Deviant sexuality in women is more passive-aggressive than violent. Some women who were denied their father's love when they most needed it may penalise other partners later. Their hostility may range from minor but frequent provocation, through verbal castra-tion (constant denigration) to more overt cruelty. Very rarely, an abused woman may physically castrate her husband, as occurred in the celebrated case of Mrs Bobbitt, who in 1993 in the USA, cut off her violent husband's penis while he slept.

Cold hostility is acted out by refusing sex, using one of several familiar excuses. Some men accept the classic 'headache', perhaps finding the reality of straightforward rejection harder to take. A genuine headache will, in fact, often be relieved by sexual activ-ity which encourages the release of endorphins, the body's self-manufacturing pain relieving opiates.

Other than in the case of Mrs Bobbitt, sexual assaults on males by females rarely make the headlines. In 1993 however, a thirty-three-year-old male executive, in a firm making hot tubs in Pomona, South-ern California, complained of sexual harassment by his employer, a thirty-three-year-old married woman with two children. In a story that inspired the film *Disclosure*, he claimed that after his employer had given him a present of two pillowcases, 'she would go into his office, close the door behind her, embrace him, kiss him and con-tinuously tell him that her interest in him was sexual'. She would also fondle his genitals. After six years of torment, he finally took his employer to court. A Superior Court jury in Los Angeles unani-mously found that he was a victim of unlawful sexual harassment. He was awarded damages of more than $1 million, the heaviest to date in a sexual harassment case involving a male victim.

Reading about male compulsive deviant sexuality may help women to be on their guard when men act out some of the more violent and dangerous manifestations of their sexual fantasies. It is sometimes argued however that accounts of sexual deviation may have an adverse influence on the non-deviant. In 1996 US film censors denied a licence to the film *Kids,* a quasi documentary covering twenty-four hours in the lives of adolescent boys and girls in New York. This showed graphic scenes of drug and alcohol abuse, rape, deviant sex and violence. The decision was made on the grounds that other adolescents would be corrupted by it. An adolescent male able to read accounts of sexual deviation or view horrific scenes of abuse, however, will already have had his sexual preferences established during infancy and early childhood. He would be unlikely to be further influenced. Because understanding behaviour is the first step towards changing it, a woman who finds her male partner compulsively repeating a potentially dangerous deviant sexual practice, will benefit from insights into his conduct. It is to be hoped that she may learn to recognise dangerous patterns and take steps to avoid remaining in contact with him. Her male partner's understanding of his dangerous compulsion will go some way towards helping him control it.

Of all sexual crimes, incest is the most socially prohibited and by its nature the most immature. Being condemned both by conscience and religion, it is also, for risk-takers compelled to challenge their consciences, the most arousing. The perpetrator is frequently a childlike and often violent male with a personality disorder. His regular sexual partner may be afraid of him and rather than face his anger, passively collude with him. If she has frequently refused to have sex with him, she may feel that she is partly to blame when he abuses their daughter who he may have encouraged to believe that it is her duty to please him. At puberty or soon after, she will begin to resent an act which she realises is exploitive. If she is too frightened to complain to her mother or to the social services, she may seek advice through organisations such as Childline. She may however love her father and despite his behaviour wish to protect him; she tells no one.

Those who abuse children are dependant not only upon their marital partners, but also on their children. Like most bigots they need a victim as a target for their prejudices. They will deny their children their rights and like tyrants everywhere, have a strong belief in the efficacy of punishment. If an abusive father's crime comes to light, the abused child's violent and abrupt separation from him will represent an additional trauma for her. Feeling abandoned and rejected, she will blame herself not only for her father's behaviour but also for its outcome. She may take minimal consolation from the belief that she is the favoured daughter, especially if her siblings are envious of her although they may also be angry that she has been singled out for the 'love', albeit perverse, which they have been denied.

Female victims of deliberate and unwanted incest have both physical and psychological wounds. They grow up to distrust men and will find it hard to form healthy commitments. Eating problems (anorexia or bulimia) in a girl who has been sexually abused are common. She will dislike her body and will fear that her developing femininity will attract further unwanted attention if not from her father then from other men. Severe weight loss leads to a return to a pre-pubertal state which will allow her to opt out of adult femininity altogether. Abused girls have little sense of their own worth and believe, incorrectly, that their slimmed-down appearance will provide them with a second chance to experience the genuine love they were robbed of in childhood. They may eventually learn in therapy to be in touch with more appropriate 'grown-up' sexual feelings. Even if they later form a stable relationship they often have insufficient self-confidence to want children of their own fearing that they might 'abuse' them as they themselves were abused. They continue meanwhile to abuse their bodies by starvation, by binge eating or by self-harming. Incest may very rarely occur accidentally. Siblings separated at birth may meet by chance and fall in love with one another not realising that they are related. A rapport so powerful and intense may occur that it will seem to both of them that they have known one another all their lives. But should they marry and have children there is an increased risk of congenital anomalies.

Paedophiles, like abusive fathers, seek positions of authority in which they may play a paternal role. Homosexual paedophiles seek to comfort something of themselves which they recognise in small boys. Initially this urge may be non-sexual, but it is one end of a continuum the other end of which is child molestation. Paedophiles are self-doubting individuals with low self-esteem, who are terrified of rejection. They feel more comfortable with children, are usually shy, self-conscious and lack social skills. They may have had a tyrannical and possibly violent father with whom they had to play the submissive role. It is this dominance/submission game that the paedophile re-enacts with his child victims.

Sometimes a paedophile will try to provide a child with 'love' through philanthropy. Not all act out their need for sexual love. Most men in this group are able to control their impulses and lead useful lives caring for children sometimes as teachers or as childcare officers in institutions. Others may seek approval from a child's parents as they once did from their own. If this approval is withheld, explosive anger may rarely lead a paedophile to attack parents through their children. In 1996, at Dunblane primary school in Scotland, William Hamilton murdered sixteen children in order to punish all those parents who had refused to allow their sons to attend his scout camp. 'If I can't have them, then neither will they.'

In Greece, in the eighth BC and for a hundred years or so, sex was subordinated to the higher value of aesthetics. The idealisation of beauty led to paedophilic behaviour becoming an official practice in some communities. It was thought that the noble qualities of a father could be passed on to his young son through peno-anal penetration, and it was regarded at the time as an acceptable practice between teacher and pupil, soldier and servant. But the present-day, legally proscribed paedophile is unlikely to make an adult sexual relationship, and will often be impotent if he attempts to do so. If hostility and hatred of self come together in him, he may be dangerous, and harm what he sees of himself in others. Any treatment, other than possibly social-skills training, is usually ineffective, since in most cases there is very little potential for positive change.

Necrophilia (sexual intercourse with a corpse) is the last resort of the sexually inadequate whose fears of rejection are absolute. *Cardenio*, a 'lost' play first performed in 1613, attributed to Shakespeare and based on a character from Don Quixote, describes the sexual obsession of a tyrannical sexual deviant who pursues a chaste maiden who in despair commits suicide. The protagonist exhumes her body, crowns her his queen, and then has sexual intercourse with her. The play encapsulates the driving need of a psychopath whose sexual obsession extends beyond the grave.

Bondage may cause sexual arousal in men who actually dislike women but not to the extent that they want to hurt them. Bondage is non-dangerous, but certainly hostile, since its aim is to prevent a woman from moving her limbs during sexual activity. A man experiences a sense of power when he controls her. The act of bondage recalls the helpless but unfulfilling attachments of a child imprisoned in a solitary confinement with a mother (the warder) as his only companion. A genuine bond with his mother at birth would have made it unnecessary for a man to tie a woman down ensuring her availability in order to re-experience it. He is in fact switching his role from prisoner to prison officer, a career choice which in reality may well be his, chosen not by him but unwittingly for him by his mother years earlier. The impotence of the 'imprisoned' child becomes replaced in the adult by power when the tables are turned. He can then control his partner by binding her as he was once 'bound'. This provides him with the child's wished-for omnipotent gratification on which he missed out but which is now aggressive and retaliatory. Its aim is to humiliate, dominate and stimulate a woman in any way he chooses. By asserting his superiority, he feels his potency enhanced. Since his sexual partner is tied up she cannot push him away, and his sense of rejection is temporarily overcome. A possibly more benevolent bondage is illustrated by the gifts a lover may give a potential bride. Necklace or bracelet – loving embrace or chained woman?

Anal intercourse usually reflects hostility to the mother. In infancy the anus is used for the rejection of feeds experienced at first as good and wholesome, but which, when the digestive process is completed, become of no further use. By using the anus instead of the vagina for penetrative sex, both partners are re-enacting memories of being at first loved, then used, and finally disposed of. By denying women their biological right of procreation, a man retaliates against the mother who, symbolically at least, once turned her back on him. Any woman, who agrees to anal intercourse, is colluding with her partner's feelings of rejection, because they correspond with her own. Similar, but more overt and more immature forms of hostility are carried out when men and women urinate or defecate during sexual activity. This act reflects the time when attention was received from a neglectful mother only when a child's incontinent needs were being attended to. An infant soon learns that the soiled diaper, an effective weapon used to control mothers, provokes an immediate and attentive response.

Spanking may also arouse some women whose wish to be beaten reflects not only a denial of their femininity but is sometimes linked with an inability to respond to peno-vaginal sex. Occasionally (invariably in fantasy), the breasts themselves are attacked. A not uncommon male fantasy in a man who has remained angry with his mother, is that of topless women taking part in a boxing match. The padded gloves that protect them from being harmed reflect the infant's puny and feeble attacks on a mother unaware of her son's feeding needs.

An extremely rare, but potentially dangerous, paraphilia is apotemnophilia in which a male becomes sexually aroused by one-legged females. A male who suffers from castration anxiety (the child's fantasised fear of having his penis cut off if he continues his love affair with his mother) is thought to be temporarily relieved of his fear when he is in a relationship with a female amputee, since he is reassured by the fact that it is she who has the absent limb (penis) not he. The condition is only dangerous on the extremely rare occasion when a man contrives to wound his non-amputee partner in such a way that amputation becomes necessary.

Erotic strangulation suicide is also a dangerous paraphilia but harmful only to the individual who practises it. It occurs exclusively in men who experience increased sexual pleasure from depriving the brain of oxygen at the moment of orgasm. The technicalities involved in obstructing one's own airway are complex and danger-ous. The sufferer from this sexual compulsion may lose conscious-ness before he is able to release the ligature from around his neck or to remove the plastic bag from his head. The coroner's verdict is 'accidental' death. Such is the public interest in sexual deviation that when those in public life succumb to this and other compulsive erotic needs they usually make newspaper headlines.

A boy is said to fear the loss of his penis if he continues competing with his father for his mother's love. He believes that his sister's (apparently castrated) genital is *her* punishment for doing so. Rather than be constantly reminded of a fate which, as a child, he supposes he only just managed to escape, the need for a fetish (a sexual object alternative to the vagina) comes about. Underwear will reassuringly conceal the vagina but at the same time (because it is likely to be transparent) draw attention to it and encourage potency. A clothes fetishist is overwhelmed by his addictive need and may be driven to stealing knickers, often from washing lines and usually at night. Foot fetishism attracts men with castration fears. They are drawn to the part of the body furthest from the vagina (the castrated genital), an ever present reminder of these fears. The foot may also recall a time when, as a child, the fetishist felt he was being 'walked over' by indifferent care-givers.

> Sebastian, a thirty-year-old man was brought up from the age of four by a smothering mother and an every-other-weekend absentee father. He lived with his girlfriend, was never certain of his true sexual orientation and was often impotent. When he was fourteen a school bully taunted him with comments about his femininity. He would also embarrass him by shouting 'I've had your mother' in the playground. He would then give him what was known in the school as a 'dead leg', kneeing him on the outer side of his thigh causing his leg to become numb. Sebastian could readily identify with the bully's views about his sexual orientation but his comments about his mother made him feel acutely uncomfortable. During his therapy it became apparent that he had taken over the role of his father who had abandoned his mother when Sebastian was four. Never having heard of castration anxiety, he was interested to discover that his 'dead limb' was the equivalent of penile castration, the legendary punishment for loving his mother and wanting to take his father's place.

There are many non-dangerous fetishes. Underwear may be eroticised even in the absence of its wearer. Skin and hair are both attractive and erotic. The first loving expression between a newborn infant and its mother is through skin contact and skin continues to play an important part throughout life from the (apparently) casual touching (often between relative strangers during conversation) to the handshake that varies from a revealing limp indifference to a firm clasp.

> Michael, a hair fetishist, was so attracted to a woman's long hair, that he was compelled to cut a lock from it whenever an opportunity presented itself such as when he sat behind a woman in the cinema. He gradually came to realise that cutting a woman's hair represented not only an attack on her 'crowning glory' but that it may also have reflected an envy of her sexuality.

Frotteurism, the harmless but nonetheless offensive rubbing of the penis against a woman in a crowded place is usually exclusive to males whose immature, timid and tentative approach to sex seldom becomes more intimate.

Exhibitionists fear rejection by a sexual partner. Believing themselves to be unattractive they are reassured when noticed and admired. Male exhibitionists are more likely to act out their needs sexually, while women content themselves with exhibiting the breast (but never the genitals) in socially acceptable situations.

A less obvious form of exhibitionism is the sexually explicit joke. The aim of the oral exhibitionist is to achieve a shocked response. Nothing can be more deflating than when the joke falls flat. Obscene internet chat room conversations may inadvertently be amusing as in the play *Closer* (Patrick Marber) in which two men talk to one another, each of then convinced that the other is female. A more threatening form of oral exhibitionism is the obscene telephone call. Heavy breathing and sexually provocative comments terrify women who believe that they have been specifically targeted.

A young man charged with this offence, described in court an incident that he had recalled when he was having psychotherapy for his compulsion. When he was five his mother worked in a shop situated below their apartment. A telephone extension connected the child's bedroom to the shop. His mother had instructed him to pick up the telephone as soon as he woke up, or if he was frightened.

Because she could not leave the shop unattended, she would reassure and comfort him down the telephone. He gradually became aware that whenever he made a phone call to a strange woman he was compulsively repeating the distanced love of his childhood. The judge's sensible verdict was that the young man should continue with his therapy. When he eventually understood that his distant mother could never have been physically close to him because of the circumstances of her life, he gave up looking for 'distanced' love via the telephone.

The voyeur, like the exhibitionist, experiences maximal sexual arousal only when the object of his interest is at a distance. He is afraid of women, and avoids genuine contact with them. The 'peeping tom' is likely to be an immature adult whose remote upbringing will have allowed only for arm's length involvement. The lonely male lurking in the bushes at night hoping for a glimpse of his beloved is a sad reflection of the child who looked longingly through the banisters at night while downstairs his parents ignored him.

The adult movie, viewed in the obscurity of the cinema or in the privacy of the home, satisfies the needs of the male, who from early childhood, accepts as his fate isolated sexual activity with no physical contact. It reflects a 'dutiful' upbringing by a mother who fulfilled her son's material needs but not his affectionate ones.

When men steal love it is called rape. When women help themselves to love it sometimes takes the form of kleptomania, the compulsive desire to steal from a shop, a symbolic provider. The kleptomaniac is seldom badly off. She envies what others possess and believes that she was denied her rights as a child. Since nothing was given to her freely, she feels compelled to steal. The high level of risk involved in stealing gratifies her, leading to levels of arousal which are sometimes sexual. Although rare, spontaneous orgasm is said to occur.

The term 'deviant' is derogatory and was coined at a time when ecclesiastical laws governed sexual behaviour. Fundamentalists of all religions continue to proscribe as deviant sexual acts which exclude vaginal intercourse, on the grounds that they deny procreation.

They also deny the existence and importance of recreational sex as an intimate form of communication in those yet to make a permanent commitment to one another, as well as to those whose age and reproductive interests make penetrative sex unnecessary. Most foreplay alternatives are generally considered a necessary and agreeable aspect of a loving relationship acceptable to those with strong feelings of mutual affection.

Every compulsively repeated sexual act in adult life mirrors specific aspects of an emotionally deprived childhood. Looking into this mirror will remind prospective parents of the mistakes their own parents made with them. Identifying the reasons for their sexual compulsions will discourage unsuitable interactions with their infants, factors that must almost inevitably lead to later disharmony.

When sexual arousal ceases to be available as compensation for love withheld during infancy, the option of buying it may appeal to the passive and is certainly more socially acceptable than stealing it.

7

Prostitutes and Their Clients

Do not profane your daughter by making her a harlot, lest the land fall into harlotry and the land become full of wickedness.

Leviticus 19:29

Women who believe that love was withheld during childhood have few options available to them. A happy marriage is frequently unachievable since the loveless tend to set up situations which fulfil their negative expectations. A woman, who has learned to cope with childhood rejection by accepting it, will often re-enact her feelings of emptiness with others whose needs echo her own. Falling in love with another impoverished victim, however, is hardly likely to be of benefit to either of them. Some seek frequent brief relationships; others who have been encouraged to look to the Holy Family for support, by parents who have recognised their own shortcomings, may rely on celibacy. The timid and self-effacing, who rate their chances of attracting long-term commitment as low, may encourage men to buy short-term gratification from them.

The prostitute, who relies on the illusory love provided by commercial sex, is expected to offer sexual encounters as a service to men, some of whom may be seeking an outlet for their hostility to their mothers or compensation for the love they were denied. Such men compulsively act out scenarios with women who are paid to concern themselves with the unfulfilled needs of their clients. Men to whom prostitutes are surrogate versions of earlier care-givers, put themselves, literally, into their hands. Inadequate and possibly intermittent comforting is now provided by an adult surrogate. The difference being that the surrogate must now be paid for her attentions.

In addition to fulfilling the expectations of her clients, a woman who sells love may also be satisfying her own needs. She extracts payment from men for the loving concern which one man – her father – should have given her for nothing. Lap – table or pole – dancers attract groups of more timid predators who are invited to look but not touch.

The illusion of intimacy between those who buy sex and those who sell it is powerful. Occasionally friendship between vendor and client may occur because sexual intimacy has been confused by one of them (usually the client) with emotional intimacy. The likelihood of a permanent relationship developing is remote, since men who use women for sex, and women who demand money for providing it, are hardly likely to enter into a relationship of mutual trust. Some prostitutes however, are so skilled at convincing their clients that they are unique – mainly because many of them want to believe it – that such relationships do occasionally occur.

Eighty-eight-year-old Victor visited the same prostitute every Thursday. He deluded himself that she not only found his visits as emotionally gratifying as did he, but that since he had pointed out to her the error of her ways she had given up all her other clients. He insisted on taking her to lunch from time to time and was oblivious to the fact that she couldn't wait to get back to work.

Substantial sums of money are often extracted by prostitutes from clients to help educate children or to support a drug habit. These extras are a bonus for the woman who learned her talents from a reluctant-to-give father who had to be 'got round' (seduced) if she wanted anything. For every woman willing to sell sex, there are always men willing to buy it. In times of economic hardship, some women work as part-time prostitutes to help balance the family budget, and others, some of whom may be asylum seekers, will be forced into prostitution to pay their pimps. In today's sexually permissive climate, a sexually hyperactive man rationalises that his brief encounter with a prostitute provides little more than a release of tension and is preferable to lonely masturbation. Others reason that if they have a live-in partner, acting out some of their more bizarre fantasies with a prostitute will protect them from revealing needs over which they are convinced they have no control, and of which they may be ashamed,

Men who make use of the services of a prostitute often express a paternalistic and hypocritical view of their actions. This represents the conflict between their compulsion to exploit women and their desire to rid themselves of it. They attempt to rescue the prostitute (rather than themselves) from an unacceptable lifestyle: 'What's a nice girl like you doing in a place like this?' The prostitute however is not interested in her client's psychopathology. Her lifestyle satisfies her childhood-driven transactional needs with an exploitive man and above all provides her with a regular income. A prostitute may sometimes be approached to satisfy other psychological needs.

Robert, a forty-five-year-old lawyer with two children, happily married and particularly religious, would periodically feel compelled to drink to excess and to seek out a prostitute. He would pay her not for sex, but for a description of her activities with her other clients. When his curiosity had been satisfied he would leave. On his return home he would be obsessed with the fear that while drunk he might unwittingly have had sexual contact with the woman and exposed himself to sexually transmitted disease. His contamination phobia was almost exactly equal and opposite to his desire to confront it. Although he would have no memory of physical contact, he would spend hours washing, scrubbing and bathing, using strong disinfectants. Once the effects of the alcohol had worn off he would experience remorse and worry that he might infect his wife. During his therapy it transpired that, as a child, Robert had been jealous of a younger sibling and believed that his mother loved his brother more than she had loved him. His questioning of the prostitute was aimed at satisfying his curiosity as to what attention other men (his 'brothers') were receiving. His fear of contaminating his wife (the mother of his children) was a reflection of an earlier wish to harm his mother for denying him her love and giving it, like the prostitute, to another. Gradually he was able to come to terms with both his fear and his anger and eventually became able to think out his past rather than act it out.

Since concern for the sexual needs of the prostitute in the sex act is essentially non-existent, most clients concentrate only on their own erotic needs. Their responses are therefore enhanced and the desire to repeat the experience self-reinforcing. Most men find it difficult to confess to their regular partner that they have unresolved immature desires and are embarrassed by their compulsion to re-enact a gratification which should have been experienced during the first years of life at the hands of their mothers.

Children's experience of love reflects both the circumstances in which it was given and the degree of attention paid to them at the time. If a mother ignores her children other than when they misbehave, then smacks and later cuddles them, they will associate physical pain with loving attention as adults. An adult who has, as a child, been constantly humiliated by his mother, may become sexually aroused by re-enacting humiliating scenes such as crawling on the floor while a woman metaphorically (and sometimes literally) walks all over him. A request to act out this performance with the mother of his children is one that few men (particularly if they have wives whom they see as extensions of their mothers) would find easy to make.

The earliest memory of Charles, a twenty-five-year-old unmarried man, was of lying on the floor at the age of four while his mother was vacuuming the carpet. She was only able to complete this task by occasionally stepping over him. He recalls that his only reason for crawling was his curiosity as to what he might see up his mother's skirt. His mother apparently was unaware of this, although she may well have wondered why he was still crawling at the age of four. He remembers feeling sexually aroused by this experience and repeating it whenever possible, either with his mother or with other women such as the cleaner. As an adult, when away from home on business, he would invite a call girl to simulate his mother's earlier activity in his hotel bedroom. His is the story of the humiliated child endlessly curious to discover what was once hidden from him.

The acting out of bizarre presexual and sexual acts with a complete stranger who has declared her readiness to perform (in the theatre of the absurd) by advertising her services in a phone booth, and agreeing to any number of (un)dress rehearsals, allows disbelief to be temporarily suspended. As in the theatre, where first night nerves are not unknown, the performance may turn out to be a flop. Prostitutes soon become familiar with the infantile needs of their clients. Their understanding of those who wish to recall episodes of childhood gratification – ranging from the wearing of rubber wetsuits to the administration of bizarre punishments – would seem to benefit both parties. But while the prostitute gains financially, her client, by reinforcing his attachment to immature gratification, loses out emotionally. His repetition of earlier erotic experiences will be to the detriment of an established, affectionate adult relationship. In the absence of such a relationship however, a prostitute provides a recreational activity that never loses its appeal. Understanding deviation will help parents ensure that their child's early presexual needs are fulfilled so that, as adults, they will not choose an activity that gets them nowhere other than perhaps to a genito-urinary clinic.

Massage parlours and saunas are popular with those shopping for sex. Full intercourse will be on offer, but such is the fear of sexually transmitted disease that it does not always take place. Some women are also reluctant to perform mouth/penis acts asked for by many men. Men are sometimes satisfied merely to watch others perform the sexual act, confirming their expectations that they are more suited to an 'off-stage' rather than to a participating role.

The prostitute occasionally fulfils an educational need. For reasons usually due to a fear of failing to live up to their partner's expectations, some men may never have achieved full sexual intercourse. Others, who are bisexual and have had no previous sexual experience, may be helped by a prostitute to adapt to a lifestyle chosen for purely social reasons. Those with a high degree of performance anxiety may find that a sympathetic and understanding prostitute will help reduce this anxiety. She will provide a 'sexual health service' in a non-demanding setting for an anxious man.

What of the prostitute herself? It is likely that she will despise a man who pays her for sex, who makes bizarre demands, who is sometimes violent and who shows no interest in commitment. Although this may be true, she will hide it from her client. Many prostitutes have regular partners who are willing to accept that their girlfriends are frequently 'unfaithful'. Such men compulsively re-enact roles in which, as children, they were treated by their mothers as inferior to and less loved than their siblings. Their resentment at such treatment becomes displaced on to the women with whom they live, whom they believe they love, but towards whom they are frequently violent. Such men have remained immature and dependent. They gain some morbid satisfaction however, from being kept by women who, like their mothers, 'love' someone else but with whom (unlike with their mothers) they can act out their anger and resentment. They frequently abuse and attack their live-in partners whom they scapegoat for the mothers who rejected them.

Both the prostitute and her regular partner have been exploited by their parents, and both are angry. Living on money extracted from men who depend on them, and for whom the prostitute feels nothing but contempt, represents some compensation for the love which was earlier withheld. The prostitute's upbringing however, may not always have been dysfunctional. Some women may have been forced into prostitution by criminals and others will adopt it to pay for their drug habit. Most will have come from a background where the father is likely to have abused his role by demanding that his daughter please him by complying with his wishes. Only if she did so would she receive the approval she craved. Reacting to a childhood in which she was expected to give her love freely to parents and receive nothing in return, she will now reverse the roles by demanding payment for her 'love'.

The prostitute expects and accepts some degree of maltreatment from her clients. Because of her compulsion to repeat her past, she will involve herself with men who exploit and abuse her. Her pimp (a prostitute by proxy) and who might be her regular partner, also exploits her by living off her earnings. Like the prostitute, the pimp has a desperate need to be loved and he too will be promiscuous and have other partners.

The prostitute uses sex as a vehicle to act out the power struggle between herself and the men who stand in for the father whom she believes did not love her. Her promiscuous search for the love she was once denied, will inevitably disappoint her and she will continue re-enacting the rejection that she experienced in childhood by turning her back on one man after another, until she is either overtaken by age or settles for a permanent relationship. Most live in hope that one day their prince will come. The fact that he never does may be because the stories which impressed them as children will have also convinced them that such a hope is only a fairy tale.

8

Nightmares or Sweet Dreams

Men fear Death, as children fear to go in the dark: and as that
natural fear in children is increased with tales, so is the other.

Francis Bacon

Unloved children do not cope well with adversity but even loved children may sometimes grow up with low self-esteem. An early influence on children is the bedtime story. Traditionally most children seem to love 'once upon a time' stories and probably welcome an opportunity to revisit the past. They may risk confusing the fictional past with their own. They see themselves either as a 'goody' such as Jack, in *Jack and the Beanstalk*, or *Cinderella*, or as a 'baddy' in the clutches of a stepmother, wicked witch or ogre. The emotional responses of sensitive children are likely to determine with which character they identify.

Stories about kings and queens (mothers and fathers), princes and princesses (boys and girls) are the most popular with children. Royalty, like parents, have absolute power. By equating a 'bad' king with an authoritarian and dictatorial parent, unhappy children may wonder whether they are in fact princes or princesses who have been abducted as babies and left on the doorstep of their parental home.

With the idea of getting their children to relax before they are left alone for the night, parents read them fairy tales and nursery rhymes by which they may be either pleasurably excited or moderately frightened. For those who suffer from separation anxiety these stories are more likely to terrify than to reassure. Alone in their beds and afraid of the dark because they need more parental input than others more robust – to enable them to cope with the nothingness and solitude that night brings – they often have difficulty in falling asleep. Separated from their parents and from the familiar sights and sounds of the day, they will be the children most influenced by the fairy tales read to them or the cartoons they watch. They are also likely to be disturbed by the aggressive heroes and manipulative heroines, who steal, cheat, rob and kill while their victims are evicted, abused, sexually-battered, poisoned or eaten.

'Jack' (the name given to a serial killer whom children will hear about later), knave and murderer, is presented to boys as a hero. This association of criminal with folk hero continues into adulthood when real-life murderers are given pseudonyms such as 'Bluebeard' or 'Black Panther'. Prince Charming, an icon promising to fulfil the dreams of every young girl, undertakes much but delivers little. Cinderella, envied for her rags-to-riches transformation, is in reality the passive victim of a cruel, exploitive and neglectful family. She may be rescued by a rich and handsome prince but if childhood patterns are anything to go by her prince (not unlike the prince of a much lamented twentieth-century Cinderella) may turn out to be anything but charming.

Cinderella's passive role is later reinforced by romantic fiction, plays and films. Fragile children on whom Cinderella has made an impression, may well believe that they can only escape their destiny if, like their heroine, they are able to satisfy either the wishes of socially ambitious parents or the sexual needs of a man. These 'Cinderellas' are content to wait for a Prince Charming to instil meaning into their lives.

Other heroines with whom small girls identify, Little Red Riding Hood, Goldilocks, Gretel (*Hansel and Gretel*) and Beauty (*Beauty and the Beast*), are all exposed to abuse that may result in death. Some children will find an echo of their own upbringing in these unedifying tales in which children (usually girls) are not only misused by parents or by those in authority, but are exposed to necrophilia and death by poisoning (Snow White), and cannibalism (Little Red Riding Hood). Could such stories encourage an acceptance of the normality of such behaviour in the minds of those already sensitised to emotional abuse?

The horrors to which young and impressionable children may be exposed, before being left alone to reflect upon them in the dark, will have an adverse influence particularly on those whose upbringing predisposes them, as adults, to find ways (sometimes violent) to shift the balance of justice in their favour. Fiction and illusion causes confusion in the minds of the very young who find it hard to distinguish between fantasy and reality.

In the past, unloved children were influenced only by fairy stories. Today the bizarre and threatening images of computer games serve as a visual reinforcement of them and are incorporated into their fantasy world. Psychologist Bruno Bettelheim argued that by separating right from wrong, and good from evil, and by using clearly defined characters that portray either wickedness or virtue, the fairy tale – enabling children to see and understand both ends of the spectrum of human behaviour – allows them to choose the role with which they identify. This may be true of loved children, but what of the abused and the vulnerable? Faced with a scenario that is only too familiar, they are provided with a script that is both easy to learn and to identify with.

Violence portrayed on television is an issue so well debated that thoughtful parents know where they stand on it. Censorship, for adults, who are assumed (sometimes wrongly) to be beyond being influenced adversely by what they see or read, is to be deplored. It is essential for young children. Children sensitised to violence by parental neglect are so readily influenced that with no yardstick against which to compare what is offered to them, they must be treated as a special case. Problems may arise when vulnerable children bond with virtual care-givers on the internet, in chat rooms or in computer games.

The fairy tale has as fixed and malevolent an influence on a vulnerable child as some of the dogma forced by 'quasi-religious' cults on the 'childlike' minds of vulnerable adults. Television programmes deemed unsuitable for young children are restricted to the post nine p.m. watershed. Violent fairy tales, however, may be read to them at any time. While it is true that no one now is likely to be exposed to the full horrors of the brothers Grimm, Hans Andersen and Aesop, children are still exposed to sanitised versions of them. While these versions appear to be more politically correct, the underlying themes remain the same: fear of spiders, falling off walls or down hills, or raking out the cinders while more favoured siblings go to the ball.

In a study published in *Archives of Disease in Childhood* in 2004, researchers found that 'broken heads, beheadings, and babies falling out of trees were a feature of many nursery rhymes' and that there was 'ten times more violence in them than in afternoon or evening television'. Acted-out versions of these horror stories in pantomimes remain as frightening today as they ever were. Exposing children to bedtime fairy tales continues to be more likely to lead to nightmares than to sweet dreams.

When unloved children watch cat-and-mouse cartoons, they will identify either with the sadistic cat (the abusing parent) or the timid mouse (the victimised child). Cat and mouse behaviour reflects a cycle of violence which may be reinforced by Punch (father) and Judy (mother) 'getting away with it' messages which children one day may repeat with their own children.

How exactly do children, whether or not they have been desensitised to verbal violence by their parents, interpret the accounts of exploitation and neglect, discrimination against women, anger, envy, greed and cruelty to which they are exposed? Messages are readily absorbed especially when they are delivered with conviction by parents on whom they depend.

Young children are incapable of evaluating or judging what is told them. They accept everything at face value. Even loving parents may fail to offer interpretations which would help children understand the moral issues which are addressed, allowing them to absorb, undigested, often paternalistic ideas inculcated with sexist bias and, by definition, prejudiced.

In a class of eight-year-olds given an exercise in creative writing by their teacher, a boy wrote of a man who was shot in the head by drunken men. He survived by eating the brains of wolves. He then cut off the heads of three random victims. Could this boy's story, a gunshot injury caused by irresponsible adults, followed by serial decapitation, have been provoked by listening to fairy tales read by well-meaning parents? Are children taught to cope with adversity by using fairy tales as examples, or does the fairy tale provide the potentially violent with a destructive blueprint which it is only too easy to follow?

Not all children have the ability to write their own fairy tales but some may re-enact them if not at once, then later in life. Bad behaviour (invariably violent and not infrequently frightening) can only be identified by a child by its effect upon others. He will not only learn to fear punishment and retribution, but possibly also take sadistic pleasure in the suffering inflicted upon wrongdoers. Since the fear of retribution is known rarely to be a deterrent, the child could be left with the impression that sadism may be linked with justice and is to be commended.

Early impressions such as these are acted out by those who later take the law into their own hands. Criminals are known to attack other criminals for crimes of which they themselves disapprove. Are these self-styled 'vigilantes' (ostensibly seeking justice for others) fighting their own wars and re-enacting the struggle between the goodies and the baddies so graphically described in the 'instruction' manuals of childhood?

Tales by the brothers Grimm describe justice and sadism in attacks upon those deemed to 'have it coming to them'. Victims of racism and sexism are depicted as unworthy, intrinsically evil, and deserving of punishment. In Nazi Germany, Jews were portrayed as 'ogres' (easily recognisable from childhood) and their persecutors had no difficulty in convincing themselves that, like the villains of the fairy tales, their victims 'had it coming to them'. The combination of horrific fairy tales, reinforced by TV violence, may also be responsible for the current increase in the incidence of knife crime by young children. In the infamous case of Jamie Bulger where a young child was murdered by two older ones, was Jamie a stand-in for a preferred sibling, or did his killers regard themselves as 'Babes in the Wood' abandoned as they were by a wicked uncle and, using Jamie Bulger's parents as scapegoats seek to make them suffer?

Unloved children will readily identify with the distorted and night-mare-like portrayals of negative behaviour (envy, jealousy, murder-ous anger and greed) which are read to them especially when their own negative feelings are suppressed by over-strict, albeit loving, care-givers. Negative feelings have as much validity as positive ones and it is entirely appropriate for children to express rage if they are kept waiting, or jealousy if they are forced to share their toys with a sibling. Envy is normal if children believe that someone possesses and withholds the love to which they instinctively know they are entitled. When parents suppress a child's negative feelings in the interests of so-called 'good behaviour', these feelings are likely to surface later, when they will have become socially unacceptable. Loved children, with warm and concerned parents, similarly exposed to the same fairy stories, will be less emotionally involved with them since they will be foreign to their experience.

In the fairy tale, chastity (sexual coldness) as well as violence is rewarded, while so-called evil, usually represented by giants and dwarfs (the victims of hormonal anomalies), is punished. The punishments are cruel (decapitation), and often sufficiently violent, to tune into the smouldering rage of rejected or abused children. Most parents would like their children to be warm and happy, compliant and loving, and to grow up (at least relatively) free from greed, envy, deceit and violence and to 'live happily ever after'. This is unlikely to be the fate of a child whose emotions have been quashed by over-discipline. The behaviour of such a child will continue to be influenced by stories in which punishments are severe and suppression of sexual feelings rewarded. The result of such indoctrination can only be harmful.

> Millie's four-year-old preschool behaviour was hard to live with. She was a fidget, always on the go and unable to sit still for a minute, particularly at mealtimes. When she was five she was diagnosed as suffering from Attention Deficit and Hyperactivity Disorder. Her easygoing mother coped well with Millie's problems but her father, himself brought up by rigid parents and unable to tolerate her typically impulsive behaviour, believed that strict discipline was in order. Millie's tears of frustration drove a wedge between her parents who subsequently divorced but were concerned that Millie should not suffer. Six months after the separation, Millie's behaviour, relieved from the pressure of her father's constant disapproval, began to improve.

Psychoanalytic theory believes that man must struggle against overwhelming odds in order to find meaning in existence. In the fairy tale the successful outcome of this struggle may involve cruelty so extreme that children already predisposed to over-strict behavioural control may be obliged to find an outlet for their feelings.

Sexist, gender-related games (dolls or soldiers), reinforced by the violence of the fairy tale, reflect the paternalistic bigotry already learned from thoughtless parenting. *Ten Little Nigger Boys,* which originated from the devaluation of blacks by white Americans, has long been banned in the USA in recognition of its violently racist content. Fairy tales also concern themselves with anti-feminist issues (the search for an obedient spouse) and class propaganda (climbing the social ladder).

Through these stories, some women, often themselves the victims of male prejudice, collude with men in indoctrinating their children with the belief that only men are powerful, and that women are possessions, whose survival depends on manual skills, physical attractiveness and cunning. Similar collusion is seen in actual cases of child abuse, where some mothers turn a blind eye to exploitive behaviour by their spouses.

The position of women in fairy tales usually written by men, is always equivocal. They are treated as prizes to be won, and are passed on from father to husband. They are valued for their physical appearance or because they possess exceptional domestic skills (cleaning, sewing and spinning). The appellation 'spinster' is still used to describe an unmarried female, i.e. a woman whom no one wants.

The steps taken by ambitious parents to ensure social betterment often carry a downside risk, with children becoming unwitting pawns in a dangerous game. This point is well illustrated in *Rumpelstiltskin*. The king offers to marry a young girl whose mother, in the interests of making a good marriage for her daughter, claims that she can spin an unreasonable number of skeins of flax a day. In the event that she will be unable to do so she agrees to the king's terms, namely that he can kill her.

When the time comes for the future queen to fulfil her contract, the frightened and exploited girl knows that she will be unable to carry out her impossible task. She is saved by a small black (evil) creature who offers to spin the flax for her. When she asks what she must pay him, the creature says that he will possess her (penetrate her) unless she can guess his name before the end of the month. Once again the girl allows herself to become a victim of conditional love and, at the same time, a seed of racial prejudice is implanted in the young reader or listener. Each evening the black creature returns with the spun flax, and each evening the future queen attempts unsuccessfully to guess his name. On the final day the king mentions that he had noticed a dwarf with a twirling tail, seated at a spinning wheel and singing: *'Little does my lady dream/ Rumpelstiltskin is my name.'*

When the black creature appears to claim the girl, she sings the rhyme to him and he flies off, leaving her possessed of the cunning and ability to drive a hard bargain. The daughter has now acquired the same characteristics as her scheming mother and is equipped to treat her own children as she was treated and to bring them up with prejudiced and distorted views – of blacks and those suffering from growth disorder.

In *Little Red Riding Hood,* a young girl takes food to her elderly bedridden grandmother who has just been eaten by a wolf. Impersonating the grandmother's voice, the wolf entices Little Red Riding Hood (using a 'wolf whistle'?) into the bed of her grandmother whom he might well have sexually abused before killing and eating her.

Goldilocks and The Three Bears, Snow White and the Seven Dwarfs, and other similar stories also suggest female vulnerability. Goldilocks is in the home of three bears. In their absence, she eats their porridge and lies on their beds. On their return, the bears threaten to kill her. Goldilocks is so frightened that she jumps out of a window and either is killed or – in another version – arrested by the police and taken to prison. In yet another version the intruder is an old woman (perhaps a mother who is no longer welcome in the home of her grown-up children). In any event, she is never heard of again. The desire to get rid of the old woman reinforces the anti-authoritarian hostility of children who rebel against cruel mothers and who as adults scapegoat other mothers.

Snow White, another innocent intruder, enters the house of the Seven Dwarfs. Like Goldilocks, she eats their food then falls asleep on their beds. Perhaps she too would have been similarly disposed of had she not been as small as the dwarfs themselves. Snow White, the 'fairest in the land', uses her physical assets to buy her freedom. Her stepmother, the queen, envies her beauty and each day asks her mirror to reveal which of them is the more attractive. The mirror cannot lie and replies that it is Snow White. The angry queen orders a huntsman to kill her stepdaughter and bring back her heart as proof that he has done so. The huntsman (like the dwarfs) is seduced by Snow White's beauty. He kills a small animal instead of Snow White and brings back its heart to the wicked stepmother. When the mirror still fails to reassure the queen, she concludes that Snow White is still alive. Snow White is in fact now living with the dwarfs all of whom have 'fallen in love' (are having sex) with her.

The queen disguises herself as an old woman and offers Snow White a poisoned apple. Snow White eats it and dies. A handsome prince awakens her with a 'kiss' (another fairy-tale euphemism for sex) and by doing so puts new life (a baby) into her. The wicked stepmother having failed to achieve her murderous goal chokes to death from rage and frustration.

Snow White not only emphasises the seductive role played by female sexual attractiveness, but contains intimations of jealousy, murder, necrophilia and paedophilia. By 'putting new life into her' the prince not only restores Snow White to life by the use of his sexual potency but makes of her an underage mother. Both Goldilocks and Snow White give children the idea that rough justice is acceptable (even before the defendant's side of the alleged offence is heard), and that it is permissible for a girl to use her sexuality to seduce men in order to obtain the love and affection denied her elsewhere.

Fairy tales introduce children to sexism, ageism, racism, envy, vanity and the pursuit of evil, all of which may appear as aspects of normal behaviour. Similar desensitisation to violence in the presence of relaxation occurs when parents allow their children access to unsuitable video material in the home environment. This acclimatises them to visual violence and reinforces messages previously encoded in the fairy story. These messages may encourage children to become immune to the suffering of others and prevent them from experiencing pity, a powerful defense against cruelty.

More violent messages are derived from the 'Jack' stories. *Jack and the Beanstalk* exposes children, who may have received insufficient counterbalancing love from parents, to ingratitude, hostility to women, murder, cannibalism and perverse sexuality. Jack sells his widowed mother's *milch* cow for a few beans. She angrily throws the beans into the garden where they grow towards the clouds like a ladder. Jack, equally angry at having lost forever the cow's milk that had kept him going after he was weaned, selfishly turns his back on his mother and climbs the beanstalk to seek happiness elsewhere. He kills a giant whom he thinks may have murdered and eaten his father years earlier and marries the giant's wife (a replacement for his abandoned mother). He lives happily ever after, having achieved premature sexual potency, presumably by stealing it from the giant.

Cinderella, a beautiful but emotionally abused, motherless girl, is also disadvantaged by having a distant, weak father, an indifferent stepmother, and cruel stepsisters. Her bereaved father has married a widow with two unattractive daughters. He does little to defend Cinderella from the hostility of his new wife. The stepmother and her daughters, envious of Cinderella's beauty, contemptuously devalue her. They give her menial domestic tasks, such as raking out the cinders, leading children to empathise with her lowly status and encouraging them to feel, as many do at one time or another, that their brothers or sisters are preferred by their parents. Cinderella, seldom allowed to forget her undervalued status, is permanently confined to the kitchen. With a passive father, and an aggressive and cold stepmother, she becomes increasingly withdrawn and depressed. When her two stepsisters are invited to a ball at the Royal Palace, Cinderella is not allowed to accompany them. She daydreams however that she has been invited. She fantasises about the mother she has lost and with whom she continues to identify (her defence against separation fears), and invests her not only with the magical powers of a fairy but of a fairy godmother. The unloved Cinderella has now acquired powerful defences against neglect and deprivation, namely wishful thinking and idealisation. She deludes herself into believing that she inhabits a magical world in which she has the power to make anything happen, including romance and sexual adventure. She imagines her fairy godmother sending her to the ball, exquisitely dressed and wearing beautiful glass slippers, in a coach pulled by white horses. She knows that she must return before midnight when her godmother's magical powers end.

Towards midnight, Cinderella becomes so preoccupied with the prince, that she almost misses her deadline. As she hurries to leave the palace she drops one of her glass slippers on the stairs. The prince retrieves the slipper and vows to marry whomsoever it fits.

Many women try on the slipper (including Cinderella's ugly sisters), but it is only a perfect (phallic) fit for Cinderella. She and the prince are clearly meant to go through life together – if not hand in glove, at least foot in slipper.

Once again the fairy godmother (Cinderella's idealised mother) steps in and restores her protégée's status from rags to riches, enabling her to marry her prince. Cinderella may now forgive her opportunistic sisters who, powerless to hurt her further, swear to love her forever. Cinderella's father, the handsome prince of her childhood, is now replaced in her fantasies by another prince. Unaware of the dangers of marrying a father figure she hopes, almost certainly in vain, that her prince will always be by her side. She is unlikely to enjoy sex with him because she will see him as a father replacement rather than as a lover. Cinderella's need to be loved however is so intense that she forgives even her unloving and selfish sisters.

While girls identify with their mothers, they will look to their fathers as role models for the partner they will later seek. The daughter of a bully will be drawn to a bully, the daughter of a weak, cold man to a similarly cold partner. Cinderella's relationship with her Prince Charming is a magical one. In real life she would probably have been attracted to a man as unavailable as her father had been. Such a man might well be involved with other women (as was her father with her stepmother) and would have fulfilled her expectations of a male partner, namely disappointment.

This immoral story continues to influence young girls who accept Cinderella as a role model. They are not impressed with the importance of being loved by both their parents (enabling them to grow up to find a fulfilling relationship with a fellow adult) and are encouraged instead to wait passively for a Prince Charming thus perpetuating their childhood expectations of exploitation. Abused children cling to the parents who have exploited them, often grow up to have personality problems and will almost certainly pass on to their children the suffering that they themselves experienced.

Beauty and the Beast demonstrates the incestuous attachment of a beautiful young woman to her exploitive father, but reveals how he is prepared to leave Beauty, his daughter, in the hands of a Beast in return for his own freedom. The Beast has captured both father and daughter and is then himself 'captivated' by the daughter who presumably uses similar techniques to those she has learned from her own abusive father. Beauty eventually discovers (but not without risk to her life) that beneath an ugly (i.e. abusive) exterior, there may sometimes be a heart of gold. This sinister message reinforces the submissive role expected of young girls, and shows how the young and defenceless may be sexually at risk from beasts, i.e. powerful and older men. It also encourages them to believe that their abusers should be forgiven because they mean well.

Fairy tales often feature helpless children who have been humiliated, degraded, and turned out of their homes by wicked stepmothers. The wicked parent is usually depicted as a (step) mother, a replacement for the 'good' mother who has died. These stories often lead to recurring nightmares of being chased, lost, killed or left orphaned which may persist in the vulnerable not only throughout childhood but also into adult life. Unloved children believe stories in which women as well as children are invariably exploited. They identify with the hero and heroine and are powerfully influenced by them. It is only when children realise that the horrors of the bedtime happenings are imaginary and bear no relationship to them that they cease to be frightened of them. If children's lives are cruel and abused however, they will not only feel unsafe in their beds, but will anxiously await the arrival of the avenging monsters and demons that they believe will harm them. Because those children 'know' they are 'bad' (why otherwise would they be treated so unlovingly?) they continue to blame themselves for the fact that they are neglected or abused by their parents.

Loving parents need not worry overmuch about whether or not their children are being influenced by violent images. It is neglectful parents who reinforce angry and fearful emotional responses to their children's unsatisfactory home environment, by exposing them to horror stories in the guise of fairy tales. No child should be so cocooned that he or she is screened from all adverse information. An awareness of the dangers inherent in the real world is essential to healthy development, provided the child is exposed to counterbalancing security at home. Children will only be compelled to re-enact the stories with which they are impressed night after night before they go to sleep, if what takes place in them echoes their own 'once upon a time' early life experiences. Mothers who are themselves self-confident and fulfilled will pass on their self-confidence to their children. But what if they are not?

9

Image Makers

To gild refined gold; to paint the lily.

Shakespeare

The question must be asked whether mothers who are over concerned with the appearance of their children want them, or themselves, to be admired. Do they fear that unless their children 'put on a good face' they will be ignored as they were themselves once ignored? Is the mother who neglects her child saying that he should be accepted for who he is rather than how he looks, or is she thinking of her own mother to whom appearance was everything and has decided to rebel? Are artistic directors whose lives are spent in promoting products in fact promoting their parents' product, namely themselves? If adults had been promoted unconditionally as children, would there be any need for spin?

The target audience for the advertising industry consists of those who were told as children that their approval rating was based not so much on if they were good, but if they looked good. For those not dependent on their looks, but on how they are, the TV commercial represents nothing more than a mindless interlude between programmes. Some may even enjoy these mini-features which they will appreciate more for the medium than the message. Those who tune into the message may gain insight into the director's own early programming because it echoes their own.

Since those in the advertising industry probably have no idea of what their parents actually wanted from them, they allow their imaginations to run riot. Using current indices of loving attention, directors have always had a field day with Freudian images. Cars paired with ice-lollies, seductive fashion models paired with seductive four-wheeled models, 'Shakin' that Ass' paired with the boot of the Renault Mégane. It has taken some time to persuade both advertisers and consumers that fast food, fast cars, and fast women are unequivocally bad for you. Since everyone knows that neither obesity, death on the roads nor sexually transmitted disease are good ideas, why do we need to wait for advertisers to draw our attention to them and for politicians to make them an issue? Is it only when politicians have achieved power that they consider social issues and, instead of addressing parenting issues, they nanny the electorate instead? Above all are parenting, power, politics, and promotion a good mix for parents and children to be involved with?

The Advertising Standards Authority has always had to deal with complaints about the motor manufacturer's association of high-performance cars with high-performance sex. Emphasis on power, speed and sexuality, which appeals to the emotionally immature, to joy-riders, and to speed record breakers has been reluctantly modified in favour of promoting environmental and safety issues.

Despite this, when in September 2006 *Top Gear* TV presenter Richard Hammond attempted to break the British land speed record on an airfield in Yorkshire and crashed at about 300 mph, he received more media coverage than did the war in Iraq. High risk, getting there first and a need for admiration appealed to many. Had they all been brought up to believe that in order to be noticed they had either to do something spectacular or at least look special?

The advertising industry attracts the acutely self-conscious, the uncertain, and those in need of care and attention. Artistic directors are for the most part unaware they are struggling to put not only the product but themselves across. By tuning into early interactions with mothers they find suitable associations with what they wish to sell. If they place too much emphasis on sexual iconography however, and not enough on the product, the consumer may lose himself in his own fantasies and the message will misfire.

Even non-sexual icons used in advertising are sometimes so powerful that they may be counter-productive. *Campaign,* the magazine of the advertising industry, points out from time to time that it is often the commercial that is remembered rather than the product. Joan Collins and the late Leonard Rossiter (in the classic ad in which, while looking at his watch, Rossiter accidentally pours his aperitif into Joan's lap) were thought by many viewers to be promoting Martini rather than Cinzano, its number one rival! In commercials, humour is frequently paired with sadism, and nostalgic dependency emphasised. A commercial for Hovis compares bread (the staff of life) with mother/child attachment, while BT's erstwhile Beattie, Maureen Lipman, as the Jewish mother always on the telephone to her children, represents attachment from a distance.

Less obvious imagery was made use of in the two-dimensional paintings on wood depicting saints and the Holy Family used by the early Eastern Orthodox Church to promote family life. Iconography focuses attention not only on the industry's 'sacred' images but acts as pointers to their commercial meaning (as opposed to their spiritual meaning) by engaging the observer's imagination. Imagery can sometimes be relied upon too heavily to hammer home the message. The name of the product is soon forgotten while the image lingers on.

In the past, consumers were offended by the overt sexual content of aggressive advertising. The ad for the computer game Earthworm Jim – 'Get your worm out for the birds' – had an arrow pointing suggestively at the crotch of a semi-naked man beneath the caption 'Not this one'. In equally suggestive commercials – such as for Cadbury's Flake – appetite for food was paired with appetite for sex. Viewers were uncertain whether they were being persuaded to buy a chocolate bar or to indulge in oral sex, the contemporary equivalent of the mouth/breast intercourse of the infant. To the creative director (whose preference is clear) the message was obvious.

The film-maker, whose parents may have emphasised feeding at the expense of other manifestations of loving attention, lingers over wrappers being 'stripped' before food/mouth 'intercourse' takes place to the accompaniment of sexually arousing music. After the food has been eaten the question of elimination must be addressed. In the TV commercial (as in real life), the disposal of the infant's waste products is dealt with by a woman. No lingering camera here. 'Mess' is quickly disposed of, and the anal associations of waste products de-emphasised. In a further exhibition of denial, puppies are used to promote lavatory paper.

While anal sexuality is socially unacceptable, phallocentric sexuality was, before the ban on tobacco advertising, openly linked with cigarettes, cigars and the lovingly polished car. The director might secretly have hoped that despite his artistic efforts the sexual component of an advertisement would be ignored (sometimes a cigar is a cigar) in the interests of truth. But the macho, chain-smoking cowboy of the early Marlborough commercials was always highly likely to end up with cancer or coronary artery disease and the attractive girl never did come with the car.

Parental care in the form of metaphor may promote enterprises such as property development and the railways. The differing attitudes of the British and the French may well be responsible for the well documented problems once associated with the Channel Tunnel. While the French readily submitted to the incursion of the rail link, the English cried 'rape', and the high-speed tracks planned to penetrate the British countryside only slowly materialised. In boom times, banks, building societies, and insurance companies, with their reassuring logos, promise concern, in the form of security, to the emotionally insecure. But in times of recession the Lloyd's horse may let you down, your assets may not be safe behind the slamming doors of the Woolwich and the umbrella of the Legal and General may not protect you from the rain.

The chronically unhappy, a group particularly insensitive to spin, may gain little comfort from it and are usually better served by the intellectual stimulus, amusement and distraction provided by the entertainment industry. The sad clown and the stand-up comic, both of whom hope that some of the happiness they generate in others will rub off on themselves, the attentive cinema and theatre audiences who are encouraged to suspend disbelief, all act as panaceas for those whose unsolicited gift was a disappointment.

The role of the paparazzi is to raise the profile of (frequently sad) celebrities. The world may smile upon them, but they dread the time when the smiling stops. Their glossy image speaks to those who admire it and both are momentarily comforted by the distant interaction, a reminder of what could have been but which does not change what is.

Those who yearn for the front page seldom rely on image alone to compensate for earlier parental indifference. Even drugs and alcohol, in addition to talent, are often insufficient and more desperate measures needed. Princess Diana's beauty, newsworthy relationships and charitable endeavours were only just taking hold before her premature death brought an abrupt end to her interest in image enhancement.

Public curiosity is persuasive, long lenses intrusive. The victims of disturbed childhoods allow the press and television into their homes. The lure of promotion is hard to resist. Parent/child interactions have now entered the kitchen where angry 'children' (Gordon Ramsay et al.) are in conflict over 'feeds'. The sexually provocative Nigella Lawson attracts more viewers than the prosaic Delia Smith, because fantasy outstrips reality. Equally informative was the TV competition between restaurateurs who vied with one another for the privilege of running a kitchen for a celebrity chef. Week after week saw the losers actually crying, if not over spilt milk at least over unacceptable food.

Those who are not helped by watching others being brave and convinced that laughing it off does not work, nevertheless continue to rely on the entertainment industry for comfort. The promise of fame, fortune and recognition draws the sad and needy to the stage, and those unable to act, but who identify with actors, to the audience. The theatre makes for anxiety amongst actors since performance is judged each day as if for the first time. The drip feed of approval – the unspilt flow – is too frequently interrupted, while the tensions involved draw the actors together and a bond is formed. They are a family.

> Minerva, a fifty-two-year-old actor, was always in tears at the end of each run, when the cast kissed goodbye before going their separate ways. She had never understood why. Her father had died suddenly when she was six and her mother was unable to cope. She gave Minerva to her pregnant sister to bring up, but her aunt's major concern was with her own baby. Minerva's understanding of life was of being loved and left. The theatre fulfilled her expectations.

The theatrical producer relies upon the artists and technicians (his family) to fulfil his emotional (disguised as financial) needs. He makes promises to them, as his own parents did to him, which he knows he may not keep. Their reliance upon him increases as they learn to accept his exploitation. On his every word hangs life (fame and fortune) or death (anonymity and penury).

The director deals with his feelings of having been insufficiently approved of in his upbringing, by working with those in desperate need of even more approval. An actor auditioning for a part knows that his acceptance will depend on his being pleasing. Since being rejected is the more likely outcome – in part due to the discrepancy between the number of out-of-work actors and the scarcity of parts – disappointment has to be the name of the game. The director will decide who will be 'loved' and who will be turned away. A 'recall' will satisfy those hoping for a second chance (to please) as he re-enacts the childhood scenario in which he seeks to replace love 'lost' through the death or divorce of a parent. This is based on the illusory belief that had the child been more pleasing he would not have been abandoned in the first place.

Music satisfies a need in those whose hunger for approval is fed by sound. Whether soothing and soporific (the lullaby), or stirring and violent (the march), it can be acoustically penetrating and sexually evocative. Ravel's *Bolero*, with its seductive beat, has been used in film (*10* starring Bo Derek and Dudley Moore), and in the 1986 Olympic World Figure Skating Championship, as a rousing accompaniment to the potent dancing of Dean with the 'ice-maiden' Torvil (the hot chocolate on the cold ice cream). The appropriately named, *Mamma Mia* rocked the audience in its cradle with the 'feel good' lyrics of Abba.

Ballet dancing, generally associated with women, displays traits by dancers of both genders of a need for mothering, as yet unfulfilled but satisfied, albeit temporarily, by movement and music. The popularity of *Strictly Come Dancing* reflects those who are satisfied with 'the vertical expression of a horizontal desire', while dancing to music without a partner, will attract those who seek harmony in the absence of physical contact.

Clive, a forty-two-year-old divorced and lonely man brought up by his father from the age of six, discovered a leisure activity in which he was able to achieve fulfilment on his own. Night after night he sought out venues where he could dance on his own and speak to no one. If someone did approach him he would chat briefly and leave. He would also dance at home but only to classical music – the early music of an emotionally silent childhood. The deaf Beethoven's *Ode to Joy* was one of his favourites. The unseen choir (his absent mother) was an essential component of his enjoyment.

Clive's brother, ten years his senior, had once told him that shortly after he was born their depressed mother fed and comforted her infant but never spoke while feeding him. She listened instead to classical music on the radio. As an adult Clive continued to seek quiet harmony. By doing something that was both enjoyable and a reminder of the time when at one with his mother, he felt comforted and fulfilled.

Clive's lonely self-sufficiency resulting from the absence of mothering during his childhood, and his reaction to music and dance as an adult was a socially acceptable comfort to him. Others may seek erotic compensation instead. Eroticism plays a major role in the entertainment industry. Its main outlets are the internet, film, or video and magazines. It is directed largely at an all-male audience and is, not surprisingly, exploitive of and hostile to women. Women, who are hostile to women, whose hormones deny them more aggressive outlets, are more likely to remain dependent on care-givers. Many will compete with other women either in fashion or in sport. Couples with emotionally deprived backgrounds may sometimes depend on pornographic imagery. Arousal levels may at first be enhanced but desensitisation to sexual stimuli soon occurs.

Bob, a forty-year-old married man, was addicted to watching adult movies. His sex life revolved around them. His wife was expected to share his interest. Over time his interest in the films faded as did his sexual responses to his wife. He was surprised that his ability to have sex with her had ceased. He was unaware that his erotic responses to screen images had overridden his affectionate feelings for his wife;

when this was pointed out to him his sexual responses to her gradually returned.

Pornography and affection do not co-exist. Many women find sexual imagery which portrays women as sex objects, distasteful rather than entertaining. Although women may be exhibitionists they are seldom voyeurs. Magazines describing sexual encounters and the problems arising from them, are however of interest to them. The late Pope John Paul II, in an annual letter to priests to mark Holy Thursday (Easter 1995), stated that 'pornography is unfortunately rampant, debasing the dignity of women and treating them exclusively as objects of sexual pleasure'. He further condemned it on the grounds that 'it does not favour either marital fidelity or celibacy'.

Both males and females report that they find the exploitation of women disagreeable. Some males, unloved in childhood, are influenced by pornographic images that simulate violent attacks on women in retaliation for earlier humiliations experienced with their mothers. Sadistic imagery, on video or in magazines, is a logical extension to the 'cruelty to children' pornography of the fairy tale and nursery rhyme. Pornography also feeds into existing sexual fantasies which are harmless stimuli for self-gratification. The high levels of arousal induced in males exposed to pornography are due to the re-enactment of the most forbidden of all sexual involvements; that of the incestuous but unfulfilling love between the mother and her infant son. Such love, appropriate in childhood, may only be experienced in fantasy in adult life when the love object (a woman) is both denigrated and devalued. The inadequacies of upbringing are so common, that the demand for pornography, once introduced into society, continues to increase and even in recession remains a growth industry.

There are arguments in favour of a more open attitude to pornography, probably on the grounds that the less forbidden, the lower the levels of sexual arousal, and therefore the less the risk of sex-driven crime. This view, although logical, did not work when cannabis was reclassified as a class C drug. It is only in the potentially violent minority however, that the portrayal of brutal sexuality in the media will feed into and reinforce destructive gratification. Like every other addictive need, sex reflects the need for a compensatory – albeit often exploitive – alternative to satisfactory mothering.

The way most people think continues to be fertilised by external influences. The emotionally deprived become confused by the mixed messages to which they are subjected. Radio and TV, theatre and cinema, newspapers and advertising, rely as much on seduction as on truth to sell products, information and entertainment. The line between information and seduction has become increasingly blurred, and as messages continue to be hammered home, with ever greater stimulation needed to attract attention, the messages become increasingly self-defeating.

Those who promote a product by selling illusions of caring, may be unaware of the adverse effects on those who accept such messages at their face value. Government health warnings make even less of an impression than macho imagery. A majority of teenagers polled in a UK survey in 1997 did not know that smoking caused cancer. The unloved and immature may see little to choose between breaking into a car or breaking open a pack of cigarettes. The teenager who once chose to believe that smoking is harmless may be the same teenager who deludes himself that making a false insurance claim is not theft. The media and parents have ambivalent attitudes towards crime, possibly because both are responsible for some of it. Crime may not generally result from reading about it, but 'copy-cat' crime can only arise from the media. Convicted criminals admit to being fascinated by media reports of misdemeanours which some have a compulsion to replicate. Those whose upbringing has been 'bad news' and who also have abnormal personalities, allow signals such as the sexually explicit photograph, to feed into their fantasies and encourage them to commit crimes against women. Crime reporting reinforces their already violent reactions to a 'criminal' upbringing. Family newspapers report family problems. By sharing these problems with millions they provide reassurance for the quietly desperate. While no adult with a reasonably secure childhood is likely to be influenced by tabloid accounts of behaviour which is criminal, bizarre or psychologically disturbed, for those whose childhoods have put them at risk, they pose a threat similar to that of violent videos and sinister fairy tales. When many people think and behave alike, having been exposed to similar childhood deprivation and also to similar reactions to it, destructive groups, often fuelled by alcohol, develop. These groups, often football fans, sometimes racists, attract those who are angry and who seek scapegoats.

10

Sex and Power

Great men are almost always bad men.

Lord Acton

The *Harmful Body Positions and Habits of Children, including a statement of Counteracting Measures* (Dr DGM Schreber, 1853) was the standard paediatric manual in nineteenth- and twentieth-century Germany. This cruel and sadistic childcare guide used by German parents for almost a hundred years may have helped turn their descendants into the Nazis who absorbed its violent message and displaced it on to Jews, homosexuals and gypsies.

With hindsight, parents may recognise the role they have played in their children's struggle for power. As far as politicians are concerned it would seem to be an entirely hands-on, or a fully hands-off upbringing that produces world leaders. Should those in government adopt the parental role? Political leaders are expected to act in the interests of the electorate, but preferably not in the same way as parents are expected to act in the interests of their children. The infidelities and sexual anomalies of those in power provide insight into parenting skills recognised by family members themselves often only when it is too late for them to do anything about it.

Should we forgive a sexual peccadillo in a politician's otherwise unblemished record as we might forgive a parent whose momentary fall from grace may have caused family upheaval? The answer is yes and it would seem likely that Lord Woolf, a liberal-thinking former Lord Chief Justice often in conflict with parliament, would support such a view. He insisted that if criminals express remorse, justice should be tempered with mercy, and recommended a reduction in the sentencing tariff. This view was opposed by those in government whose own shortcomings may have influenced more condemnatory thinking. A Home Secretary with a conscience is to be admired, but a Home Secretary whose conscience is so harsh that he not only feels obliged to challenge it but is over-condemning in his attitude to delinquency in others, should look for another job.

In August 2004 it was revealed that the divorced Labour Home Secretary David Blunkett had had a three-year affair with Kimberley Quinn, a twice-married mother. Prime Minister Tony Blair, possibly taking into account that the blind David Blunkett who was sent to a special school at the age of four, lost his father as the result of a work accident and believed himself to have been damaged by the withdrawal of affection in his childhood, took the view that the Home Secretary's private life was his own business. He did not comment on the reasons for David Blunkett's draconian views on crime and punishment.

Although as children, some politicians (in the past usually members of the Tory party) may have been left in the care of nannies, many would affect to despise the concept of the nanny state. The self-sufficient attitude which tends to govern their public lives, contradicts their apparent need for extra-marital nanny-style comforting in their private lives. The Labour leadership, particularly those from homes where lack of money may have posed more of a problem than lack of adequate mothering, is more likely to comprise politicians whose compulsive need to 'put the world to rights' has driven them to the top. When the middle- or upper-class politician cheats on his wife, he will be looking for love, whereas the dishonest politician from a less privileged background who turns to fraud is seeking security.

When the late John Profumo (Harold Macmillan's Secretary of State for War) resigned from the government on 5 June 1963, he admitted that he had lied to parliament about his involvement with Christine Keeler, a twenty-one-year-old prostitute. Keeler was considered a security risk because she had also been sexually involved with a known spy, Eugene Ivanov, the Soviet naval attaché in London. John Profumo, married to the actress Valerie Hobson, held one of the country's most powerful and prestigious cabinet posts. He was driven to commit himself to a complicated and highly dangerous sexual intrigue of which the downside risk would be the end of his career and possibly of his marriage. Such a gamble seemed unworthy of consideration when weighed against his social status and his position in government. But Profumo was playing for high stakes. His need to return to a childhood that he believed still owed him something was so obsessive, that value judgements based on reality were not made. The compulsion that drove John Profumo towards his dangerous sexual liaison provides a clue to understanding the behaviour of other powerful men. Many of these men, apparently leading happy, fulfilled and highly successful lives, may, in reality, be suffering from the effects of not good enough parenting. Whilst this may have driven them towards positions of power in the first place, their role of parent figure to the voters, who depend upon them to represent their interests, cannot always be sustained. Deceiving their 'children' (as their parents once deceived them) they revert to their role of unfulfilled child and seek comfort once more in the arms of a surrogate (nanny). Profumo's tragedy has stayed in the minds of the public, not only because of the high-profile, high-society intrigue that helped sell newspapers in 1963, but because his story – repeated on several occasions since by other well-known public figures – touched on feelings with which many identified and can still identify. Members of the public are as fascinated by the sexual intrigues of politicians as they are by the sexual behaviour of their own parents.

That so many public figures were also involved in the Profumo scandal (albeit in walk-on parts), coupled with the underlying psychological reasons for his high risk indiscretion, appealed to those who had similarly been 'locked out of the bedroom' by parents who may have been loving each other, but were not seen to be loving their children. The media fed into this morbid curiosity with revelations of parties where semi-naked girls, acting as waitresses, served the (oral) needs of MPs, and whipping (naughty boy) orgies took place. Why was it that Profumo became so passionately involved with a girl not of his class? What was the significance of the whipping orgies and the semi-naked waitresses? Why did Profumo, who had married an actress, love her, convert her into a mother, then turn away from her? These events mirrored the formal upbringing to which Profumo, and others of his background, would have been exposed. The girl 'not of his class' represented the nanny with whom from birth he would have had a loving, hands-on relationship and who assumed day-to-day responsibility for his well-being. The whipping orgies – using other women as scapegoats – reflect a symbolic act of retaliation against his mother since as a child, his mother had 'turned her back' on him. He scapegoated his wife (another mother) by symbolically turning his back on her during his sexual involvement with Christine Keeler.

The drive towards power and approval (initially to impress his mother) took John Profumo to the top in public life. When circumstances forced him to abandon his compulsive childhood needs and face the real world, he immediately resigned his job. Essentially an honourable man buried under the emotional baggage that informed his upbringing, he devoted himself to helping the poor (other victims with whom he readily identified) for nearly forty years in an attempt to expiate his guilt.

A popular limerick of the time summed up the public's expectations of honesty and integrity in their political leaders:

'What on earth have you done?'
Said Christine
'You have ruined the party machine
To lie in the nude is not at all rude,
But to lie in the house is obscene.'

When John Profumo died at the age of ninety-one in 2006, politicians from all parties paid tribute to his work for charity. His downfall continues to be of interest. Old Etonian Boris Johnson, then Vice-Chairman of the Conservative Party, Shadow Arts Minister and the popular editor of the *Spectator* was sacked by the leader of the party Michael Howard, not for having had an affair (Michael Howard himself had married his mistress) but like Profumo for lying about it. Can a lying politician be trusted? Or should the electorate have admired Profumo for lying to protect the integrity of his wife and his mistress. Does this mean that adultery is acceptable in political leaders provided that they readily admit it but that different rules apply to the rest of the population?

Truth is an essential ingredient in political decisions and the absence of it in our elected leaders is unacceptable. On another level, however, the examination of inappropriate behaviour in high-profile families – the minutiae of which are reported daily in the media – throws light, although second-hand, on parent/child inter-actions. Those who deny any interest in the behaviour of public figures have either had a near-perfect childhood and therefore do not need to revisit it, or find their pasts too painful and are unable to face reminders of them.

In October 1983, Cecil Parkinson – former Chairman of the Con-servative Party and at the time Trade and Industry Secretary – was forced to resign after admitting an eleven-year affair with his sec-retary Sara Keays. Parkinson, later to jilt his pregnant mistress, was being groomed as successor to Margaret Thatcher, who knew about his affair but who (as she did with John Profumo) stood by him. In a radio interview in 1993, after a silence lasting ten years, Parkinson made three points about his relationship with Sara Keays. He said he could not understand why he had begun the affair when life was going so well for him; that his work had distanced him from his three children and from his wife; and that since the dramatic break up of the affair, he had found communication with his family much improved. Like other ambitious men, Parkinson had his eyes firmly fixed on the career ladder. His ambition devoured everything in its path, but the new car, the new home, and the new woman were swiftly followed by loss of power, loss of status, and loss of acquisi-tions before he had the good fortune to be reunited with his family and children and given a second chance.

Twenty years after the Profumo scandal, infidelity (without the lie) appeared to be both understood and condoned by the House. After a period on the back benches, Cecil Parkinson returned to the cabinet as Energy Secretary. His mistress, Sara Keays, who had been conveniently forgotten, was silenced by court orders until, in 1996, her struggle to cope unaided with Parkinson's brain-damaged child was revealed. Profumo and Parkinson both managed to seduce women and the public (at least for a while) and contributed to the general devaluation of family life, as well as undermining their own successful careers. Profumo never returned to public life and

Parkinson, having become a life peer in 1992, returned to politics in 1997 at the request of the Conservative Leader William Hague.

In 1992 another government minister, David Mellor, lost his job because of his three-month affair with an actress. At the age of forty-three, Mellor had just been appointed to the new post, Secretary of State for National Heritage, when he commented to the Prime Minister, that life was now 'going to be fun'. It was not long before the truth of this statement became apparent. The nation's heritage, which he had agreed to nurture, became confused with his own heritage as he acted out his dependent need for two women, a mother (his wife) and a nanny (his mistress). A taped telephone conversation revealed Mellor to be having an affair with Antonia de Sancha, an out-of-work soft-porn movie star who was six feet tall and described as 'nervous and flighty like a loose horse in the Grand National'. Press reports of Mellor's 'nursery games' – including being spanked by Antonia whilst wearing a Chelsea football club sweatshirt – seemed to have little effect on John Major's support for his friend. Like others before him, Mellor tried to bluff it out, and Major told him 'to tough it out'. But by now the tabloids had begun to juxtapose Mellor's sexual indiscretions with his support for a privacy law, the purpose of which was to prevent the press from publishing personal and intimate details of an individual's private life. It was at this point that 'sex, lies, and audiotape' were coupled with the damning revelations that Mellor had accepted the hospitality of a woman whose father had supported Saddam Hussein at the time of the first Gulf War. He was dismissed on the grounds of political foolishness, naivety, and the worst (parliamentary) sin of all, lying. In 1992, Paddy Ashdown, the leader of the Liberal Democrats, was reported to have had an affair with his secretary some five years earlier. He admitted immediately that the information was correct and that his wife knew all about it and had forgiven him. Parliament did the same.

Hypocrisy is unacceptable in political leaders. In late 1993, in a hoped-for but vain distraction from the many other problems that his government was facing, John Major's policy unit produced a particularly inept memorandum entitled *Back to Basics* which encouraged respect for family values, self-discipline and the rule of law. This noble, but psychologically flawed edict backfired on John Major (known as the grey man of British politics) only a few weeks later. In January 1994, Tim Yeo, the Minister for the Environment, pre-empted the publication of a story in the *News of the World* by admitting adultery with thirty-four-year-old Tory councillor Julia Stent (with whom he had a five-month-old baby). Because Yeo paid lip service to *Back to Basics*, while at the same time attempting to conceal his actions from parliament, and worse because he failed to admit his misdemeanour until he was found out, he was forced to resign. It was not until former MP Edwina Currie's diaries, serialised in *The Times* in September 2002, revealed her own four-year affair with John Major that the Prime Minister's insistence on the importance of family values took on a more retrograde meaning.

Other parliamentarians, also forced to resign, were shortly to discover that the fallout from the combination of poor parenting and political power was 'unacceptable' to the public, not on the grounds of morality, but on their need to keep hidden, information about their own early lives. A particularly sad outcome of the need for love in the guise of sex was the lonely and accidental death of a popular Parliamentary Private Secretary from cerebral anoxia due to the injudicious use of partial strangulation (an extremely risky procedure) as an aid to the enhancement of orgasm. Was he unconsciously re-enacting being squeezed 'half-to-death' by an intermittently loving care-giver?

Men with sexual fantasies so compulsive that they are unable to resist recreating the childhood scenarios from which they originated, are obliged to act them out with women other than their wives. Their exaggerated respect for their marital partners (usually mothers) is a reminder of the relationship they once had with their own mothers. Christine Keeler, Antonia de Sancha and Sara Keays are replacements for earlier care-givers who loved their nursery charges and did everything for them (presumably including occasionally smacking them while they were wearing football jerseys). The 'remote' mothers of such men were looked up to, respected and worshipped from a distance, but were unable to provide their children with the hands-on love to which they were entitled. Their legacy was a ruined career.

An honest man with sexual needs that are not dangerous should try to resolve his problems with his partner in private, rather than with the electorate in public. Whether in politics or in marriage a dishonest man should never be trusted.

Henry Kissinger's much quoted assertion that 'power is the ultimate aphrodisiac', made at the height of his political career as US Secretary of State, re-affirms the correlation between political power and the need to be loved (usually confused with the need for sex). Power in the absence of sex may be fulfilling to a few, but sex without power is the hallmark of the unloved. Power, fame, sex and money – synonyms for love and greedily sought by those in public life – are illusory substitutes for good parenting. Political power may be a turn-on for the psychologically impotent, but it is poor compensation for the absence of constancy of maternal care. Infants who have to overcome their mother's reluctance to supply them with the love to which they are entitled, will be compelled, as adults, to repeat this struggle. If they are convinced that they were given as much love as they needed, rather than as much love as their mother thought they needed, they would not have to seek confirmation of their worth later either from status or from illicit sex. Since Henry Kissinger's remark is just as likely to refer to women aroused by power as to men, politicians will never be short of willing partners with whom to re-enact their early needs.

Adulation, demanded from, and received by, politicians and pop stars, boosts both the male and female ego. The positive feedback loop, between a man's drive for power and a woman's response to it, ensures its perpetuation. The more absolute the power of the politician, the more overwhelming are his sexual needs. There is little evidence to suppose that the opposite is true for the female politician. The male hormone responsible for sexual desire (testosterone) and present at a lower level in females is known to be hypersecreted in non-human primates following social triumphs. Research has yet to confirm whether sexual desire correlates with ambition in humans whether male or female.

As male politicians climb the career ladder, their power increases, and with it goes an increasingly grandiose, but illusory, sexual potency. The urge to affirm that one is in reality on top (particularly where there is uncertainty as to its validity) necessitates the frequent seeking of confirmation of it. Politicians have more to lose from the consequences of deviant and/or extramarital sex than others. For the power-hungry, risk-taking politician, the higher the stakes, the higher the levels of arousal. Enhanced sexual response in adults, as compensation for the shortcomings in the unsolicited gift of childhood is the reward for the successful delinquent, but despair and ignominy is the price paid by the unsuccessful one.

Competitive and ambitious men need to be reassured of their status and power. Politicians only find this reassurance at general elections. For many, five years (in the UK) and four years (in the US) are too long to wait. For both men and women, the sexual equivalent of position and power may be tested with a sexually reassuring partner. Many men are often unable to distinguish between being 'on top of the job' and being 'on the job'. Successful sex serves not only as an affirmation of potency, but is also an agreeable recreational distraction from responsibility. Enhanced potency is a weapon with which politicians attack those with whom they are in competition, whether members of the opposition, or the deceived husbands of their sexual partners.

Male politicians may not always have sufficient self-confidence to test their potency against their rivals, preferring instead to make a conquest with women. When such battles succeed it reassures the victor that he possesses high levels of aggression and power, and the conquered that they have a powerful protector. As the politician's influence wanes, he will seek reassurance that he still possesses sexual potency and will attempt to recharge his failing political batteries through sex, a psychosexual and possibly biological necessity.

Increased sexual activity correlates with drives such as ambition. It is used by political leaders to provide an increased sense of power on the way up, and compensates for the loss of it on the way down. Absolute power, found when the rights of the opposition have been successfully eroded, sometimes precludes the need for sexual activity altogether. Tyrants, often the victims of an abusive childhood, are aroused sexually by brutality, none more so than Adolf Hitler, Josef Stalin and Mao Zedong. These despots suffered from the perversion of lust murder, albeit by proxy. That sexual arousal can be provoked by murder is confirmed by the manic excitement of religious fanatics when carrying out massacres. Laventry Beria, Stalin's secret police chief, acting out his rage at not having been the preferred sibling, is said to have stolen love from other children by raping schoolgirls in the Lubyanka prison in Moscow. His wife Nina refused to believe that, at the height of his political power, he had been unfaithful to her with 760 women.

Chairman Mao, another deprived despot, not satisfied with having his potency confirmed by one woman, had sex simultaneously with three or four at a time, preferably his social and intellectual inferiors, until well into his seventies. Posing as a feminist, this commander of an army of female concubines had always protested that pre-revolutionary customs, including the exploitation of women as either sexual objects and/or domestic servants, were now past. Not for him. Dr Zhisui Li, Mao's personal physician for twenty-two years, claimed in his memoirs that he was a god and that 'it was a glorious thing for a girl to go with him. If he asked a girl to go to his room she would not refuse'. Dr Li, who died in February 1995, had kept diaries on Mao's activities in which he described Mao's unsavoury personal (nursery) habits and his voracious sexuality, echoes presumably of childhood appetites which had remained unfulfilled.

In 1993 it was revealed that another world ruler, Leonid Brezhnev, although neither a Stalin nor a Mao, had also abused his absolute power by demanding that his security services kept him constantly supplied with women, in his case flight attendants. These surrogate care-givers would have satisfied his earlier childhood needs by living up to his expectations that like other care-givers, they would be here today and gone tomorrow.

Political beliefs, usually distorted by tyrants, do not in themselves seem to be a factor in grandiose sexuality. Hitler on the right and Stalin on the left, both exhibited God-like delusions. The delusion of absolute power makes potency-testing unnecessary, since the chemistry of mania – the extravagant and hyperactive behaviour that is associated with grandiosity – invariably leads to hypersexuality. Biologically speaking, the more frequent the sexual activity, the more male sex hormone is secreted. Sex steroids promote a sense of well-being. This accounts for the frequency with which power-hungry and competitive men and women, who have a compulsive urge to get there before the next 'man', abuse them. When female athletes abuse male sex hormones (an unhealthy example of penis envy) there are usually disastrous biological consequences. It is often hard to distinguish drug-abusing female weight-lifters – increasingly remote from their femininity – from males. Demigods may sublimate their drive for power in politics or sport but like some heavy-weights they may be sexually impotent. There have been many impotent political demigods, whose frequent testing of their sexual inadequacy correlates with their political inadequacy.

Hypocrisy, from which few can claim immunity, is universally condemned, and political and public figures who practise it are fair game for newspapers. The combination of sex and power amongst politicians in the USA arouses much the same interest as it does in the UK but with more emphasis on the use of well-timed revelation as an electioneering weapon. The smoking gun – or in US election speak the smoking bimbo – or even the wet condom, was used against Bill Clinton by his political opponents. American politicians, both male and female, project a greater aura of potency than their British counterparts. This may be because they are paid more or because women are more aggressively integrated into American political life. They demonstrate the same power traits as their male counterparts and assert their rights to the same 'privileges' whether economic, social, financial, sexual, or criminal. Reactions to sexual revelations in the Western world have been so dulled by repetition, that the public often becomes bored with – and worse, immune to – accounts of sexual infidelity. If the national conscience becomes apathetic and non-condemning this could have serious consequences, not in the increase of dangerous sex crimes (carried out by psychopaths), but in sexual promiscuity which corrodes family and public life. The knock-on effect will be felt by children influenced, although not always adversely (sometimes they react *against* immorality), by dishonest parenting. In 1992 Governor Bill Clinton was elected in spite of, or perhaps because of, the overwhelming number of his alleged sexual misdeeds both past and present.

Desensitisation to the concept of marital infidelity, coupled with the charisma and political competence of the candidate, allowed this to happen. Not content with rocking the democratic political boat during the election campaign however, President Clinton's political enemies continued to make allegations about his sex life (mainly in right-wing newspapers) after he had been elected. Mud-slinging is a political weapon and even the suspected sexual offences of political opponents are seized upon.

In past campaigns, presidential candidates would not have been able to withstand the smears, the innuendos – and in some cases the facts – with which Governor Clinton had to contend, and at the same time become successfully elected. Bill Clinton's well publicised affair with White House intern Monica Lewinsky during his second term as president, not only made little difference to his public image but in fact may have enhanced it, suggesting that either the American electorate was beginning to understand the significance of a disturbed childhood or more likely that it had become immunised to and bored by accounts of multiple infidelity. Bill Clinton's affair aroused maximal interest but minimal condemnation at the time although some have claimed that his wife's failure to win the democratic nomination in the 2008 primaries was because a significant section of the electorate did not want the Clintons back in the White House.

During the Kennedy era, responsible authority ensured that very little of the scandal that is now public knowledge concerning John Kennedy and other members of his family, including his father, was shared with the electorate. The press looked the other way. On one occasion in 1962, Adlai Stevenson was visiting JFK's suite in the Plaza Hotel, New York, when Marilyn Monroe was seen waiting for the President in an anteroom. When Adlai Stevenson left and Marilyn Monroe stayed behind, it was not reported in any American newspaper. John F. Kennedy's addiction to sex was such, that if he was deprived of it for twenty-four hours he would complain of withdrawal headache. Sex addiction (welcomed by errant husbands who have been offered a respectable medical diagnosis behind which to hide), a disorder gifted to them by indifferent mothers, is now considered such a problem that in-patient management of the condition is offered in private psychiatric clinics. It is treated in much the same way as other addictions such as alcohol, drugs and gambling.

JFK's behaviour was so phallocentric that sexual activity would often take precedence over affairs of state. In his biography of Jackie Kennedy, *A Woman Named Jackie*, C. David Heymann claimed that Kennedy had left an army officer holding a bag containing nuclear codes while he spent time at a sex party. It was not the first occasion on which the nation's needs had taken second place to its leader's sexual ones. JFK's younger brother, Edward, also had prodigious sexual drives. He enjoyed group sex at parties and is said to have enhanced his sexual responses with cocaine and amyl nitrite. The two brothers had much in common. They shared similar sex and power drives but more significantly, they shared the same mother.

More than forty years after JFK, extramarital sex has become less newsworthy. This is not because the press keeps the public in the dark, but because constant exposure to it has dulled the response of newspaper readers. Those whose behaviour patterns are firmly established are unlikely to be influenced by sex scandals, although inadequately loved children, whose views are still being formed, may well be influenced by them. That sex and power are inevitable components of high political status is now beginning to be accepted. Libido and the drive for power cannot be separated and together they can be a force for good, as well as a force for evil. But most would agree that politicians who possess this energy have a responsibility to harness it and to use it to further the national interest. Those entrusted with power (who speak for those unable to speak for themselves) too often find difficulty in controlling, and often even difficulty in recognising, their frequently dangerous cravings for love, sex and domination, to which their early life experiences have conditioned them. While the party in power strives for ever greater levels of achievement in order to satisfy the electorate, the opposition claims to be repelled by but may well be envious of revelations of their opponent's sexual appetites and indirectly their political ambitions.

The compulsion to succeed is a powerful defence against the fear of failure. What goes up must come down. The dreaded nightmare for the power addict is loss of status, loss of approval and worst of all, loss of potency. It is sexual indiscretion in government however (hardly a new phenomenon) that continues to exercise the militantly righteous whose wish seems to be to remove eroticism from public life. When politicians violate moral codes they have been elected to maintain, the voice of public disapproval is led by newspaper editors who are themselves men of power. Distrust and hypocrisy make cynical bedfellows.

Not everyone who is power-hungry has the talent to reach the top and not everyone equates power with potency. Everyone is entitled to a lifestyle that suits his particular talents. Understanding the power of parenting will increase the likelihood that children will choose careers that suit their talents rather than as a reaction to adverse parenting.

11

Time In

Square Pegs and Round Holes

You can't decide to become a writer as you might become a doctor or a plumber. Long before you have a conscious choice; it has been made for you.

John Fowles

Seeds sown in infancy quickly produce shoots, and even pre-school children are made aware by their parents of where their future lies. Photographers and artists look but don't touch; film directors, airline pilots, captains of industry and army officers control and direct. Fashion models, actors and politicians sell themselves; policemen and fund managers are concerned with security, but with whose security? Were the parents of all of them detached, demanding, unrewarding or unsure of their role? If so the apparent self-sufficiency of their children reflects an inner uncertainty that they could not look to their parents to put right but hope to remedy through their choice of career.

Parents unaware that they have already influenced their children's futures frequently enquire of them what they want to be when they grow up. The answers are revealing. Children may say that they want to be fire fighters, astronauts, celebrities, airline pilots or waiters. If their choice is doctor or nurse and they want to 'make people better', could it be their own 'suffering' they wish to alleviate? Is the would-be astronaut looking forward to the time when he can put as much distance as possible between himself and his apparently secure base? Has the would-be waiter been trained, by a lazy mother, to fetch and carry? Parents seldom pay much heed to their children's replies. They should. It is through their interactions with their children that they may have pointed them in one direction or another. Those who understand the significance of parental influence on career choice, might not only change their own lifestyle to one more suited to their talents, but will acquire insights which will enable them to become better parents themselves.

Adults seek to reassure children – and themselves – about what the future may bring. Children do not need this reassurance. They believe themselves to be immortal and were they able to verbalise their feelings might ask their parents to decode the hidden messages they communicate. It is only when parents allow their children to develop at their own pace, and provide them with the support and information on which they depend, that their future life-choice although inevitably shaped by parenting influence, will be one that they will come to as a result of informed decision. In the absence of this ideal, children whose emotional needs are unfulfilled will grow up to seek compensation elsewhere.

Workaholics, striving desperately to please, manifest symptoms of stress – irritability, exhaustion, restless sleep and over-sensitivity to criticism – echo the feelings of frustration experienced when their parents expected something from them before they were capable of giving it. Career choice should be dictated by an ability to understand the events which drew them to the job in the first place. By asking themselves what they are doing and why they are doing it, they will be examining their childhood needs and their parents' reactions to them and will find clues that will help them better to understand their own parenting role.

A fulfilled adult does not need to repeat a happy childhood. 'Those who do not remember the past are destined to repeat it' may be a truism, but it is a key to the compulsive repetition of behaviour patterns. Would the historian, whose upbringing was truly fulfilled, feel the need to revisit the past? Would travel writers choose to spend hours in lonely hotel rooms if their home life had been more convivial? And whose security does the insurance salesman really want to protect, his clients' or his own? Job satisfaction is likely to be an exact reflection of parent/child satisfaction.

It might be assumed that by the time the medical student has come to the end of his training he will have made an informed decision as to the speciality he wishes to pursue. This assumption may be incorrect. There are of course many reasons why doctors choose to do what they do. They range from the absence of job vacancies in the field that interests them, to a natural curiosity to learn more about a disorder that he, or someone close to him suffers from. All other things being equal, however, it is remarkable (and informative) how often the chosen speciality is driven by past interactions with parents.

Does the anaesthetist choose to work with patients who are unconscious because he expects his words to fall on deaf ears, just as they had done during his childhood or because his parents had so little feeling for his needs that he is driven through a desire for role reversal to choose a job concerned with the absence of feeling in those who depend on him? He may also enjoy manipulating his equipment which – like the patient (and his parents) – neither hears nor answers back. Despite his need to be controlling – the technique learned by neglected children to input from parents that should have been given them as their right – his patients may rely on his skills, since he will be as concerned for them as he is for the dependent part of himself which he sees reflected in them.

While the anaesthetist is concerned with absence of feeling, the cardiologist's may sometimes overwhelm him. Curious as to what makes people 'tick', he spends his life working with 'broken-hearts'. The heart (like the mother) is the life source and while he will be concerned with his own affairs (of the heart), should he have any, the heart he is most concerned with is that of his mother, whom he may possibly have thought loved his siblings more than she loved him.

The thin-skinned, hypersensitive dermatologist is likely to spend as little time with his patients as his parents did with him. Were they more concerned with how he looked rather than how he felt? If so he may find that spending too much time with his patients gets 'under his skin'. A few moments is often all that is usually needed for him to arrive at a diagnosis, and unless there is a hidden agenda such as the presence of another disease process, what you see is what you get.

Unlike the dermatologist whose parents may have been concerned mainly with his appearance, the gynaecologist's mother may have loved him and left him. He repeats similar uninvolved 'love them and leave them' encounters with other 'mothers', as one woman after another colludes with him in a brief relationship. As an obstetrician, he will feel at his most powerful and (vicariously) creative. His 'romance' with his patient begins during the first three months of her pregnancy. When she becomes a mother he will abandon her as his mother may have abandoned him when his own younger sibling was born.

There will always be women with whom he may re-enact his child-hood-driven needs. If a patient in labour requires a forceps delivery, her baby – the helpless victim of an instrumental hug – will remind him of the time when it was he who was the victim of a mother's cold embrace. Carrying out a hysterectomy on a woman may be for some an act of revenge equalled only by the gratification experienced when ter-mination of pregnancy followed by sterilisation is performed. Could this echo what he might have wished to have done to an unwanted sibling as a child, denying at the same time his mother's biological right to another child?

A female obstetrician feels at one with a woman about to give birth. She will be in touch with the brief moment when she and her own mother were inseparable. Some female obstetricians extend their need for female closeness to same-sex relationships. Dependency and hostility are closely linked, and the female obstetrician, like her male counterpart, may find some emotional fulfilment in many of the painful procedures asked of her.

The oncologist, over-protected by perhaps anxious parents, grows up to see disaster everywhere. Seeking a cure for cancer is his defence against the ultimate catastrophe, death, and no one will be more dedi-cated to succeed than he.

The psychiatrist is involved with the emotional, rather than the physical. His concern is with the self. But with whose self is he con-cerned? If he has yet to resolve his own problems, he will be unlikely to resolve what he sees of them in others. His emotional responsibilities are unique. Very rarely professional boundaries may be crossed and a patient comforted sexually. Some psychiatrists delude themselves that such advances are welcome and fall in love, not with the patient but with what they see in them of the dependent and frightened child they themselves once were. Those who sense this possibility avoid involvement with patients by treating them with distancing physical methods, with drugs or shock therapy, or in groups using the group members as chaperones. Some, in the guise of counselling, may give advice based on their own unresolved difficulties.

The radiologist, not unlike the psychiatrist, wants to find out what goes on 'behind the façade'. He may have been brought up to feel excluded, and unable to cope with emotional involvement uses the imaging screen as a shield. He hopes that by means of technology, he may be able to penetrate the barrier behind which one or both of his parents seemed always to be hiding. With reservations about his own feelings, he is nonetheless curious about the feelings of others. Once settled into his career he discovers that the truth is to be found neither in imaging nor imagining, but in a genuine and trusting relationship with another adult.

The surgeon also probes beneath the surface, but his feelings are more controlled than either those of the psychiatrist or the radiologist. He is always ready to excise the 'malignant' and there is little likelihood of reasoned debate leading to the resolution of a problem. His willingness 'to cut it out' may echo the roar of an angry father when the behaviour of a child, if not malign, was definitely bad.

Dentists, other than perhaps paediatric specialists, are usually male. Their first involvement, like that of all children, is an oral one. Most adults have moved on from the breast/mouth stage of development and their orality comes into play only in the presence of food, speech or sex. The dentist's involvement with the mouth is ongoing. He is preoccupied with the health of the oral cavity, the effective functioning of the teeth, and the bite. But what of the biting anger associated with it – the earliest manifestation of an infant's reaction to unsatisfactory feeding, the biting of the hand (or the breast) that feeds him? Was he brought up to suppress his anger, i.e. to keep his mouth shut, when his oral needs were neglected? If so, he will have found a fulfilling and profitable way of dealing with his past by silencing every mouth other than his own. If the dentist's needs continue to be fixed at the oral stage of development his attachment to the breast will still be very much part of his adult life.

Medical specialists are dedicated to their chosen field. By interpreting the metaphors associated with their work they will understand why they behave as they do. They will then be in a stronger position to consider the symptoms of aberrant behaviour not only in their patients, but also in their own children. Some use this awareness in the interests of the public through their work in the social services. A rare few (from Crippen to Shipman) overcome by grandiose ambition, misuse it in the interests of their distorted psychopathology.

Career choices are often based on low self-esteem. The exhibitionist may flaunt his penis and will expect women to pay attention to it. But while exhibitionism is an aspect of virtually all forms of performance there are more sociably acceptable ways of achieving gratification. The female exhibitionist has no desire to display her vagina but may draw attention to other parts of her body. She may exhibit her breasts on the beach or if she is in Brazil, where motherhood is more heavily sanctified, she may display her buttocks instead in the minimalist tanga. The need to be admired by men may also be satisfied through fashion, tabloid, or nude modelling. The desire to be looked at – often heavily defended against by compulsive modesty in many women – usually only temporarily improves self-esteem. If a woman sees herself as essentially unlovable, the quick fix of admiration will do little to alter her convictions. She will remain over-preoccupied with her appearance and may try to change how she looks by bingeing, starving or through cosmetic surgery. She may also become sexually promiscuous, seeking from one man after another the love and admiration which during her childhood should have been hers as of right.

> Nanette was an attractive twenty-two-year-old who had run away from home at fifteen to escape from her abusive father. She hated her body and began abusing it by cutting it and pulling her hair out. She was introduced to table-dancing by another girl. A year passed before the only too obvious positive reactions to her appearance by her male clientele convinced her that she must be attractive. She was only then able to give up self-harming. She left her job but continued servicing the needs of others by becoming a nurse.

Unlike the fashion model who seeks recognition using body language, actors verbalise their needs. On radio they experience a dual satisfaction. A child who was once expected to be seen and not heard, will now be heard but not seen. Actors play many roles, but the one they play best is the autobiographical one. If they are type-cast, it is because they are able to play that role with feeling. They may be unaware that the story is their own but they are drawn to roles that echo their life story. Their narcissistic personalities often associated with a characteristic grandiosity which obscures their self-esteem, will demand that they be admired.

As children, actors were expected to earn parental love through performance, either at school or on the sports field. As adults they will therefore distrust unconditional love, and boost their low self-worth by 'putting on a show'. Never having been loved uncondition-ally, they will be sensitive to rejection and prone to stage fright, afraid of not pleasing the audience who they fear might turn away from them. Rarely, a theatregoer will act out similar childhood problems. Resenting the attention the actors receive they will deal with their own feelings of rejection by failing to return after the interval and depriving their 'rivals' of attention.

The actor's social relationships are likely to be affected by their need to be loved. Unable to believe what others tell them, they will seek frequent reassurances that they are attractive. An actor addicted to attention often confuses it with love. Sex becomes the nurturing illusion to which they will turn at ever decreasing intervals and is used to please a partner – whom they may not love – in the hope that they might eventually come to be loved by them.

The barrister's apparent confidence and verbal skills may seem to distinguish him from the actor, but both are equally self-conscious. His quest for truth, coupled with his need to be heard as well as seen, is an echo of a childhood in which being allowed to speak only when spoken to, was a condition of parental acceptance. He differs from the actor who is usually only articulate when words are put into his mouth by others.

Unlike the actor whose need is almost entirely for emotional acceptance, the barrister seeks intellectual acknowledgement. He would have been brought up to believe that love and acceptance, rather than given freely, had to be earned. Structure and order, the result of too rigid an upbringing, will be important to him. Unless he had as a child satisfied the expectations of parents and teachers, he will regard himself as a failure and imagine that the case he is pleading is not just the client's but also his own. Reacting with anxiety to the judge's authority and seeing him as an extension of his father he may ask for mitigation. His pleas for justice or mercy would have been learned years before by memories of earlier sentences imposed upon him by a father who not only laid down the law but was both judge and jury. The barrister may experience high levels of anxiety in court through identifying with his clients, particularly if he believes them to be guilty. The unresolved anxiety left over from his childhood would be better suited to childcare cases, where he would be able to plead for what he himself wanted as a child; that is to be cared for, not only by his father but also by his mother.

Some barristers may misuse alcohol before appearing in court in order to relieve anxiety. Others attempt to avoid feelings of guilt by seeking the illusory safety of working for the Crown Prosecution Service, on the basis that if you can't beat them then join them. The barrister owes his verbal skills to a close bond with his mother. At her breast he will have learned babble talk, the essential precursor of articulate speech. Although his mother would seldom have chastised him, she might have relied on 'wait till your father comes home' tactics to discipline him. By unconsciously recalling his own early-life experiences, the barrister hopes that the charges made against his clients will be set aside.

Anxious when confronted by male authority figures, he may gradually acquire arrogant attitudes as defences against these anxieties. These are self-defeating and seldom of help. The roles will be reversed if he eventually sits on the bench. The former victim is now the judge. If in time he is made a Lord of Appeal, the illusion of absolute authority may finally reduce a life-long anxiety to manageable levels. The barrister will seek comforting relationships, often with maternal partners, in which they hope to re-enact their experiences with their own mothers. If his early relationship with her was too all-embracing, he will expect more of the same with adult partners who may not always be aware of his needs.

The barrister often has a harsh and condemning conscience which makes it difficult for him to be unfaithful to his partner. Should he decide to challenge his conscience however, extremely high levels of arousal will occur. It is for this reason that those whose duty it is to uphold the law will sometimes involve themselves in activities outside it. Occasionally a barrister, who cannot bring himself to have an affair, may solicit a prostitute solely to question her about her clients. It will be an affair by proxy, reflecting a wish to find out what went on behind the closed doors of his parents' bedroom.

While the fashion model, the actor, and the barrister need to be 'looked at' and to impress, the photographer's need is to look. Voyeur and exhibitionist need one another. Without the other neither would exist. The photographer and the model often form a passionate, but usually short-lived involvement, sometimes of love but more often of hate. Men who seek admiration have usually been deprived of it, and those whose mothers loved them from a distance are unlikely to get close enough to a woman for her to provide it. Since neither the photographer nor the model will have experienced anything other than arm's length love from either of their parents, neither of them will find it easy to express genuinely loving feelings.

The photographer's long lens gives only the illusion of proximity but he deludes himself that he is close to his subject and behaves accordingly. Addicted to admiration, his model responds. When both realise that the game they have been re-enacting is an illusion it comes to an end. The press photographer, usually male, is a more active voyeur than the studio photographer. He re-enacts his life-long desire to look through the keyhole into the bedroom. With his camera he is virtually in bed with those whose privacy he invades. The longer the lens the more potent he feels. His 'closeness' to his subject however, does not represent genuine potency any more than it does to the equally voyeuristic readers of the tabloids who look at his photographs. Shooting celebrities, however, who have achieved the attention for which he has always longed, is a gratification to which he may become addicted. He seldom considers that the invasion of a woman's right to privacy is an unwanted intrusion, a form of rape.

The window cleaner's working life is also spent on the outside. He is separated from the home and what goes on within it by a fragile, but inviolable barrier of transparent, usually dirty, glass. Although he cleans it and is able to look clearly into one home after another, he belongs in none of them. Never 'at home' in his job he re-experiences the exclusions of his childhood. He is likely to have wanted to break down similar barriers between himself and his parents, but will not have succeeded. His cleaning work satisfies his expectations of being left out (in the cold) reflecting the 'look but don't touch' interactions of his upbringing. Through his choice of occupation, balanced on a ladder, he senses that his childhood needs never 'touched' his parents. All his involvements will be distant. Like every voyeur, the window cleaner may fear intimacy, believing that his illusions could easily be 'shattered' by a reality as disappointing as that of his childhood, when his love objects were physically close, but emotionally distant.

The film or theatre director recreating his early life with his mother, controls his new 'family', as his mother once controlled him. He expects love and affection from his actors and in return he gives them the support they crave. The conditional love with which he was brought up is projected on to those who now depend on him and whom he will only 'love' if they please him. An actor, usually female, who may have been emotionally or sexually abused by her father and who has been brought up to expect victimisation might encourage the director to behave as her father did and imagines that she will lose both the director's approval and her job if she does not cooperate with him. The abused child who wants to please, and the 'father' who exploits her, come together to re-enact their respective pasts. The director's potency is enhanced when he has a compliant victim. In the absence of such a victim he may find it difficult to play the parenting role which he demands of himself and which the actors expect of him. He may make a successful marriage, but only if his partner – typically an actress – allows herself to be manipulated by him. More usually he will have a series of abortive relationships with women whose need for a 'father figure' is as intense as his own.

The airline pilot believes that his authority should never be questioned. Only the air-traffic controller may tell him what to do. He will double-check everything on the flight deck. He cannot trust others. His job suits him because in it he is able to reverse the dependent role that he played in childhood, feeling comforted that so many depend upon him. Unable to delegate, he knows that if he is to satisfy his unfulfilled emotional needs, he must not only be authoritarian, but also manipulative and seductive. If take-off is delayed, he will empathise with the frustration of the passengers but will momentarily be in touch with his urge to retaliate against parents who kept him waiting and who he believed had no time for him. Omnipotence and grandiosity will compensate him for what he was denied. His self-sufficiency obscures his passionate need for a love that was never freely available. He will need women to love and admire him and there may well be at least one member of his cabin crew willing to fulfil this need. His craving for love is food-related in the air and sex-related on the ground. At the end of the flight both these appetites may be satisfied by the flight attendant, who will have been brought up to serve and who will fulfil her own nostalgic need of being at one with a male authority figure, in a romantic setting, after an exotic meal.

Airlines have come to recognise behavioural patterns in employees whose unconscious career choice insists that they go through life with their head in the clouds. By frequently switching crews, management hopes to avoid the inevitable consequences of emotional entanglements, damaging not only to marriages (the older airline pilot is usually married), but also to efficiency, and not least to passenger safety.

The fashion designer and the hair stylist are driven neither to control nor to perform. Their aim is to satisfy two closely related needs in women. The first is to enhance their looks and the second is to comfort them. Both callings attract men and women who in other circumstances could equally well have been working in the caring professions. The caring role is essentially a feminine trait and it is not surprising therefore that hands-on caring attracts women and (homosexual) men whose closeness to women was at its most intense with their mothers. The homosexual man is able to use his caring to good effect in his work. As a child he sensed his mother's need to be loved. As a fashion designer he will bolster the needs of other women by helping them, or their environment, look more attractive. As a hair stylist he has 'heterosexual' contact with his female client. This relationship is acceptable and both feel comfortable with it. The part of the body with which he is involved is far removed from the 'threatening' female genital. He is in intimate contact only with hair, the 'crowning glory' through which women display their sexuality. More time and money is spent on hair – cutting, colouring, highlighting and blow-drying – than on any other aspect of a woman's appearance.

The female fashion designer sees her clients as extensions of herself. She is involved as much with vicarious self-gratification as with pleasing her clients. She is interested in same-sex friendships, although very few manifest same-sex preferences. Her asexual enthusiasm for women clients in the work environment may often be more intense than her sexual enthusiasm for her male partner in the home.

Nicky, at twenty-three, had found her forte as a beautician. She had grown up with an alcoholic mother who when drunk was a tiger, sharp and denigrating. Nicky's parents separated when she was six. She did not like her stepmother but it was not until she grew up that she realised that she did not like women in general. Working as a manicurist (smoothing away sharp claws) gave her a much wanted control over women and redressed the balance of her childhood.

The beautician's relationship with her client will be same-sex but non-sexual. If, like Nicky however, her relationship with her mother was poor and her client has also grown up to feel that her own developing sexuality was ignored, they could find in one another the 'bosom' friendship which they should have experienced in the first few months of life. A rapport, based on loyalty and trust develops between them and is renewed at each visit. This relationship – same-sex but sexless – gratifies them both.

The long-distance lorry driver identifies with the potency of his vehicle. He 'looks down' on other road users and understanding their frustrations and weaknesses rises above them. As king-of-the-road he needs to be of, but not necessarily with, others. A desire to follow one's own path is characteristic of the overly independent, and a defence against loneliness. At the beginning and end of the day, the lorry driver reverts to being one of the others with whom he may socialise in the motorway café. But they are ships that pass in the night: there if he needs them but by keeping them at a distance he sustains the illusion of independence for which he was praised as a child. With his libido and power invested in his vehicle, he has little time for anything but 'love them and leave them' sex. Should he find a partner who cannot cope with intimacy they would be well suited.

The car salesman (traditionally male) is attracted to the trade for reasons that vary as to whether the cars he sells are new or second-hand. Some of his clients may fantasise about power and display competitiveness and grandiosity. It goes without saying that the pleasure derived from owning and cleaning this male symbol of power is masturbatory. Self-gratification is quickly achieved and as quickly lost and fades with repetition (constant polishing). Those who change their cars frequently enter into similarly brief, but highly dependant liaisons with their gratification salesmen, as do substance addicts with their suppliers.

Those who sell new cars have a good reputation with the public and the trade. They are able to share vicariously in the potency of others and because of their high levels of integrity and honour, are not involved in commercial promiscuity. The new car is pristine, untouched and virginal, and the salesman's ambition is to deliver it as such into the hands of a careful owner. He is likely to be as faithful to his partner as he is to his clients, but since his involvement is for the most part with men and cars it would not be surprising if he were either gay or dependent upon self-gratification for sex.

The used-car salesman, like the new-car salesman, experiences the car as a potency equivalent. Unlike his new-car counterpart, however, his concern is with the cars of previous owners. He accepts that they will have been through many hands and promiscuity – often more mechanical than genuinely caring – may become the name of the game. It is not surprising that some second-hand car dealers have acquired a reputation for both commercial and sexual infidelity.

The architect, uncertain of his potency and believing that there is no one to please but himself, will expect his steel and concrete 'erection' to be admired. A few female architects, possibly envious of male sexuality, try to emulate their male counterpart's apparent potency and are increasingly seen on hard-hat building sites, but understandably have difficulty in identifying with phallocentricity. They are more likely to concentrate on residential interiors as they attempt, vicariously, to put in order a home that in their own remote past might have been chaotic.

Writers fear exposing their innermost thoughts to others. They cope better with 'fictional' accounts of their feelings. They anxiously await a positive response from readers and reviewers. Some writers use a pseudonym and only reveal their true identity if their work has not provoked the disapproval they have been brought up to expect. The writer's story is one to which they believe no one has listened. Wanting to explain themselves they believe that their spoken words will, as in their childhood, continue to fall upon deaf ears. By committing them to paper, they are obeying parental insistence to remain silent. They hope that their feelings, hitherto unacknowledged, will finally be understood. The blank page is their confessional. In recalling and rewriting their story, they are free to unload the negative feelings which they had to suppress in childhood and which as an adult may have made them prone to depression. These feelings – rage at being misunderstood, jealousy of siblings, 'greed' because of a hunger postponed to accommodate parental convenience – may manifest themselves only in later life. Therapy may be avoided (wrongly) for fear of destroying creativity, since it is usually only through their work that writers may exorcise their self-hatred. In common with other depressives, writers may be less concerned with sex, than with the love and affection denied them by the parents whose demands they were unable to satisfy. The written word reflects the unspoken protest of the once suppressed and oppressed child. It allows the writer to confront childhood authority, no matter how crushing it was at the time.

The insurance broker persuades others to buy peace of mind, but may have failed to achieve peace of mind himself. Childhood loss – the divorce or the death of a parent – may lead to a lifetime of unacknowledged grief. Selling insurance to others allows him to cope better with his own feelings of loss. This will not prevent him from re-experiencing the anger he may have felt at the time. This anger might once have been absorbed in aggressive sport – football or boxing – but as these outlets gradually cease to be available he may scapegoat others, experiencing them as the parent who had earlier abandoned him. Once retired and no longer providing others with the security he was himself denied, his own losses may need to be addressed.

The accountant searches for security and stability, not only in his client's books but in his internal balance sheet. He will not allow himself to take chances since an element of risk would not only upset the fine balance of calculation but could end in a loss that he will spend his life trying to redress. His concept of generosity may differ from that of others. For everything he gives he will expect an equal amount in return. He does not donate but invests, fearing the loss of security and love which he equates with money. He will seldom be either imaginative or artistic because his responses would be too unpredictable. He will value precision even in his leisure interests.

The accountant will perform for his clients as he was expected to perform for his parents as a child. He will identify with their needs, and do what he can to increase their wealth (since he believes that money equals love) through tax avoidance schemes and other recommendations. Advisory, controlling, often grandiose and using patronage as rationalisation for manipulative behaviour, he will act towards his clients as his parents acted towards him. His ego, inflated by the innumeracy of many of them, gives him the illusion of power over those whom he has encouraged to depend on him. In reality however, he may be sexually passive believing that he has contributed enough to an unloving past through industry and hard work, to be anything other than an armchair romantic.

The antique dealer, the historian and the archaeologist are concerned with the past. While the antique dealer and the historian live in it, the archaeologist will be 'digging it up'. All three are preoccupied with what went on earlier. It seems likely that those who look for what *was*, rather than for what *is*, believe that they have lost out on an essential ingredient of their own past. Their ongoing sense of loss may lead to unhappiness and resentment. All have a dependent, occasionally depressed, and often aggressive need. Typically their distanced parents might have handed them to surrogate caregivers soon after birth, and perhaps later sent them away to school before they were sufficiently self-confident and secure to cope with separation. Such a child's anxiety levels would be increased by life at boarding school with even more distant 'parents' (matron and patron). Unable to revisit their upbringing they will instead research the ancestral lifestyles of others.

The property developer, like all businessmen, typically searches for security. When money is cheap and property values soar, his sense of security increases concomitant with his wealth but when debts mount and wealth decreases, a feeling of inner poverty and rage about the 'injustice' of it all may overwhelm him. His legitimate activities are often attacked by some ecologists whose own destructive impulses (against which they are heavily defended) may be projected on to him. What may be considered destructive by some but creative by him does not preclude other forms of hostility. A quest for concrete development may go hand in hand with emotional conquest. Because of the relentless sex drive of the players in this industry, economic disaster – such as a fall in property values – is often not recognised until too late. Negative equity and a limp penis often go hand in hand.

The role of the teacher is to care for children and help them to adapt to life outside the family. School should be a home from home and sensitive teachers recognise that in conjunction with caring parents they reinforce the support that all children need. Most small children feel loved by their teachers and learn to share this love with other children. Jealousy, envy and the occasional violent outburst, normal amongst siblings, is dealt with in the classroom without the pressure of family expectation. Teachers encourage the gradual nurturing and development of the emotions of children, rather than abandoning them to seek a not necessarily happy compensation, in their later choice of career, for their possible suppression at home.

Those who have been cared for materially but not emotionally will grow up confused in their attitudes towards others. They will often amass possessions as others, more certain of the inadequacies of their upbringing, collect relationships. Those who have been abused may grow up to abuse others. The unloved may hate themselves and the insecure will seek security through acquisition. Many will follow careers which they believe will make up for earlier deficiencies, although they are more likely to perpetuate them.

12

Time Out

Leisure

All intellectual improvement arises from leisure.

Samuel Johnson

Leisure time, or time out, is a carefree alternative to the day-to-day disciplines of time in. It is voluntary, unpaid and available in one form or another to everyone. It is pleasurable and passion driven. It takes a unique form and can provide information on life events in childhood. Time out activities are individual specific; one person's leisure activity will differ from another's. Which activity will be chosen is likely to be predicated in childhood, usually by mothers rather than by fathers, and in ways not immediately obvious.

Many parents expect their children to share their own leisure interests and are disappointed when they do not. But a father who kicks a football in the park with his son will not necessarily turn him into a footballer; encouraging an anxious child into the local pool will not produce a long-distance swimmer; and no amount of holidays spent on the ski slopes will ensure that a child develops a liking for winter sports.

Infants who fail to overcome the reluctance of their mothers to respond to them, however, may later be drawn to conquer peaks, sometimes as distant and as cold as they may once have found their mother's breasts to be. The enthusiastic skier seeks the high levels of arousal he once hoped to find in her arms and as he skis down icy slopes can easily become addicted to his search for it.

Paul, a thirty-year-old only child of divorced parents, had been married for four years before his wife Marina, a child psychotherapist, reported certain idiosyncrasies of his that were troubling her. He would often leave the room while she was in the middle of a conversation. Whenever she brought up an issue he would react as if she had not spoken. He seldom showed his feelings and his sex drive was low. Although he was not gay he related better to men. His passion was skiing.

Marina was on the verge of divorce when her husband sought professional advice. Paul hated his mother who had been indifferent to his needs. He was brought up by a nanny and sent away to boarding school at the age of seven. His urge to conquer icy peaks seemed likely to echo memories of his cold mother. His wife felt that she had been left with no other option than to try to make up for what his childhood had denied him, or to leave him. A motherly woman, she decided to help him realise that not all peaks are icy.

If the ski enthusiast fails to make his symbolic conquest, the downside will be disappointment and loss. A default option for some is to seek alternative highs in the temporary arousal provided by food, alcohol and sex, but despite the hot meal, the warm wine and the welcoming arms of the chalet girl, the vacuum left by a mother's coldness will draw him to return time after time to the mountain, hoping that the forever out of reach peak might one day 'at least meet him halfway'.

The chalet girl may be expected to play a part in consoling the disappointed skier. She will have her own reasons for wanting to spend the winter months attending to the (holiday) needs of others. If she has been brought up to expect commitment to fail, she will not be disappointed by short-term liaisons. She may even enjoy the mother/child game and will provide her clients with comforting feeds when they return exhausted by their failure to alter the course of their personal history. She may be happy in her maternal role but is likely to refuse sex with a small boy over-compensating for his lack of mothering by drinking too much.

Unlike the skier, who has never given up on his aim to convert the cold breast of infancy into a more welcoming equivalent, the beach enthusiast chooses to wait for the sun (the life source), and possibly a woman with similar needs to comfort him. Singles' holidays, for some synonymous with sexual hyperactivity, appeal particularly to those without regular partners. These holidays are sometimes regarded as dating agencies. Unattached adults, like unattached children, search for a previous love that was never entirely available. Their demands may be intense, but even if they find what they are looking for, they are unlikely to recognise it. Their needs are so addictive and insistent that common sense, together sometimes with the precautions necessary to prevent unwanted pregnancy and sexually transmitted disease may be set aside.

Advertisements for 'singles' holidays' often carry very little information other than the unspoken promise of 'sea, sex and sun'. Beach holidays in the company of children, especially in family accommodation, are noted more for the absence of, rather than the presence of, intimacy. Buckets and spades, the gender-related beach games of children, may provide pointers to a child's future expectations. Boys dig holes while girls fill buckets. Will the sand-diggers of today become the gold-diggers of tomorrow building castles in the air in which they will never live unless their upbringing was built on firm foundations?

Flying gliders satisfies those who wish to be as 'high as a kite' (insufficient input in childhood), while scuba-diving explores the depths (of despair) to which a child may have sometimes been subjected. Bungee jumpers and mountaineers (risk-takers) look for the elation which will momentarily relieve their ongoing feelings of childhood loss. All of these activities may reflect disappointment with life as it is, because of life as it once was.

Gardening, listed as the number one leisure activity in the UK, appeals to both the creative and the destructive. While the sowing of seeds and their subsequent flowering echoes nurturing needs, the aggression involved in the pruning of shrubs and trees suggests other urges. Does the felling of a tree represent (as Freud believed) an unconscious retaliation against a powerful father who has frustrated his son's wish to cut him down (to size) and claim the love of his mother?

Children are seldom interested in caring for plants, not because they are experiencing growth at first hand but more likely because they are intolerant of delayed gratification. The child who is happy to wait is not the one who was kept waiting long before he was capable of understanding the meaning of patience. The adult male however, enjoys gardening as an agreeable adjunct to retirement. His time, previously controlled by his parents and later by his employment, is now his own. Another advantage of gardening is that it takes place within the boundaries of the home. An infertile woman unable to produce the flowers of her womb may grow the flowers of mother earth. If she has children who have left home, she is able to find a happy and creative post-menopausal extension to her mothering skills in the garden. In the latter half of his life, a man's role may be financially less certain, but with (phallic) spade, however, and appropriate fertilisation, he will be able to prepare a satisfactory environment in which to bring up his second (floral) family.

The leisure centre caters for those who want to improve their health and perhaps enhance their attractiveness. Many embrace violent exercise in the hope of delaying morbidity and even mortality. Occasionally the gym may pose a hidden threat.

> Michael, a fifty-two-year-old, unmarried taxi driver, was unable to enter the men's changing room because it provoked a compulsive urge to look at other men's penises. He was so afraid that someone would notice what he was doing that he would get changed into his gym things at home. It became apparent later that it was not the changing room that he was avoiding but his own unacknowledged homosexuality.

While ballroom dancing is enjoyed by both sexes, aerobics (in the form of dance) appeals mostly to women. Both men and women are concerned with feeling good and being fit but the quest for fitness may go hand in hand with other addictions (alcohol, tobacco, drugs or excessive eating) despite their incompatibility with body and stamina building. Many unable to cope with their addictions, particularly to food and alcohol, hope that burning calories through exercise will allow them to continue with their unhealthy lifestyle. Needless to say it will not.

Although the sexes might 'work out' together, men and women

remain emotionally apart and cross-gender communication whilst using gym equipment is virtually non-existent. Attitudes to the use of the machines (both men and women seem sometimes to be engaged in an imitation of sexual intercourse) are clearly gender-related. Some men react to the equipment as if it is a dominance/submission contest which they believe it is their duty to win whereas women often accept a more submissive role. Some women, using lighter weights and increased repetitions and often dressed in skin-tight, provocative, yet at the same time concealing, leotards, rock to and fro in the mechanical embrace of a machine. Oblivious to the sexual signals they are sending out, they may alleviate the boredom of the exercise bicycle by reading a book or a newspaper at the same time – possibly an accurate reflection of their responses in general. A male health freak will occasionally experiment with dangerous anabolic sex steroids (available for purchase at disreputable gyms) in a vain effort to attain both sexual dominance and a hoped-for improvement in his often low self-esteem.

Car cleaning, as a hobby, has little other than a clean car to commend it. It is repetitive, often compulsive, sometimes competitive, and invariably tiring. So much has been made of the significance of the car as a phallic symbol that many men, made self-conscious by their public display of lonely sexuality, choose the car wash (the motorist's equivalent of the massage parlour) where away from the voyeuristic stares of the neighbours, washing and polishing may be more comfortably enjoyed.

Those whose psychosexual development has been temporarily arrested at the oral stage, may find that eating in public, a legitimate leisure interest, particularly with an opposite sex companion, is as embarrassing as having sex in public. This embarrassment is associated with high levels of anxiety and often persists until underlying sexual problems have been resolved. After a relationship is established and sexual interest has become more genitally focused, eating with a partner may become not only pleasurable, but an indication of the state of the relationship. A selfish eater, unconcerned with his partner's predilections, is more likely to be an inconsiderate lover. Those who concern themselves with their companion's choices and even add titbits from their own plate are likely to be equally attentive to their needs in bed.

The restaurant is a convenient and socially acceptable leisure venue for those embarking on a new relationship. Both parties may be hoping that lunch or dinner will be followed by sexual activity. Since eating and drinking commonly precede the sex act (as do the satisfaction of the infant's oral needs his later genital ones), it is entirely appropriate to engage in oral activity before proceeding to penetrative sex. In the early stages of a relationship it's often bed before food, while in an established relationship it's likely to be food before bed.

> Suzanne, an attractive twenty-five-year-old unmarried woman, had since puberty been unable to eat in public. Her confusion between her oral and genital appetites was such that being watched while eating was the equivalent for her of being watched during sexual activity. Her unrecognised and denied need for mothering once acknowledged and eventually resolved, allowed her to separate her appetites and overcome her phobia.

The appetite for food and the appetite for sex are closely integrated and a preference for certain foods often points towards an individual's sexual preferences. Bland food is linked with unadventurous sexual responses, while spicy or exotic food, suggests equally spicy sexual responses. A liking for nursery food suggests sexual immaturity, a failure of early maternal commitment and a subsequent lack of readiness to enter into later ones. Greed should not be confused with appetite and is likely to be a reflection of emotional hunger. Neither preoccupation with food nor sexual greed makes for harmony. Shared and varied tastes are the best indicators of a satisfactory relationship.

'Watching television' – like car washing and working out – is a moderately addictive but essentially non-stimulating leisure activity. It may reflect a childhood in which the so-called good baby ('he never troubles me') is left to his own resources long before he is ready to do so – perhaps having been left in his buggy in the garden for too long, with the consistent inconsistency of leaves fluttering on trees as his sole companion.

Television is a socially acceptable pastime for those without a partner, or for avoiding contact with a partner by those who have nothing new to say to one another. A favourite TV programme may be seen as an alternative sexual object and is often resented by the neglected partner. While the male addict's attachment to the television set becomes increasingly hostile when he buys into adult movies (often after his partner has gone to bed), the female addict's attachment is more often to soaps and the shopping channel.

> Dana's lifelong eating disorder had led to a skeletal appearance and had brought her on more than one occasion to the point of death; she binged on TV clothes-shopping but never on food. Her fear of food, initially aimed at making herself sexually unattractive to her abusive father, was exactly equal and opposite to her addiction to the shopping channel directed towards making herself sexually attractive to her husband.

The pub and the wine bar are socially acceptable meeting places. After a few drinks in an informal setting, in which the dominance/submission aspects of a new relationship may be established, couples are able to get over any initial anxiety. Drinking together appeals to those uncertain of each other's feelings. Although one partner may insist on buying the drinks, the other may be equally insistent on paying their share. The noise level in the pub acts as a welcome barrier. Under cover of this barrier personal subjects may be discussed in relative privacy. The proximity in which a couple find themselves may also help to break down physical barriers. The pub provides a good primary meeting place. While 'Let's go somewhere quiet' is a not always an acceptable suggestion at an early stage in the relationship, the public house is a rehearsal for the private house which, with all the members of the family beneath one roof, has the potential to do the same.

The cinema, in which the inarticulate allow the actors to speak for them, is for those who find communication difficult. In the cinema couples converse in body language, starting with hand holding, as a preliminary test of the relationship. They may also demonstrate their immature oral needs, by consuming the popcorn, ice cream and confectionery more appropriate to children. A slow and considered oral stage often bodes well for the later genital stage.

Leisure interests, which may be as compulsive as sport but lack the competitive edge, once established, rarely change. Many of these interests are a testing ground for secondary courtship, in which couples re-enact some of the deficiencies in the primary courtship (with the mother). This allows them to gather information about one another, an essential prelude to the development of a relationship.

13

Sporting Chances

Although good parents love their children and are attentive to their needs some children may still lose out. Their choice of sport as adults provides them with a chance to win out.

Only losers need to win. Winners have already won and have no need to challenge a team, an adversary, a weight or a clock. Winners do not have a strong wish to overthrow powerful rivals or demonstrate their uniqueness and value. They already have a sense of worth and are happy with the knowledge that their parents thought them unique.

Winning, when applied to upbringing, is not an absolute. Winners can, occasionally, also be losers. Provided losing occurs infrequently and is never a feature of loss of parental love, it is part of normal development and an essential ingredient of learning strategies. Nonetheless the power and potency, unique to winners, are components of the unsolicited gift.

Not many sportsmen realise that as they 'tee-off', 'line-up', 'kick-off', 'go first', 'sail close to the wind', 'skate on thin ice', 'dip their oar in the water', 'paddle their own canoe', 'put their ball in someone else's court' or 'keep a straight bat', that their choice of sport is the logical, albeit coded, but never satisfactorily concluded, ongoing conversation they had with their parents years earlier using body language. It is important that parents understand what their children are saying and to realise how they might have unknowingly influenced them. Decryption may be too late for the misunderstood victims of their upbringing but not too late to avoid them influencing their children. Their children's choices will not be determined by frustration and misunderstanding but by more appropriate factors such as talent and determination.

Team sport involves same-sex players. It attracts those who, often with low self-esteem, find it easier to express their feelings if others are around to support them. The group's involvement must of necessity be gender specific if only for reasons of physical balance. Each member of the team relies upon the others in his struggle to win. They are a family. A band of brothers. A football, whether kicked or thrown, evokes identifiable responses in both spectators and players. A goal scored, outwardly a mere test of skill, is followed by ecstatic leaps, hugs from the 'family' and support from the fans in a demonstration of brotherly love.

In sport, love between brothers is acceptable, overt homosexuality is apparently not. When football star, Justin Fashanu, disclosed his homosexual preferences, after years of top-class national and international football, he was subjected to abuse from both players and spectators. He later committed suicide. The implication that a footballer is gay is still considered by players to be the ultimate insult. When Graeme Le Saux in *Left Field* (his 2007 biography) wrote that in 2000 David Beckham had called him a 'poof', following an episode on the pitch, the reaction in the football world was as intense as it had been seven years earlier. Violence, on the other hand, is accepted and even admired – provided it does not hold up the action. When, in January 1995, Manchester United's Eric Cantona famously leaped into the stands and kicked a verbally abusive spectator (who clearly did not love him), he had the sympathy of both players and supporters. Management however, obliged to work to a different agenda, grounded Cantona for eight months.

The football fan is usually a male. He empathises with other fans and with the players and becomes absorbed into the 'family' group. What the group feels, he feels. What they do, he does. When his team loses he feels powerless. When they win he is elated. When they score so does he. His screams of joy are shared with his siblings and with the (parental) manager. It is platonic love and hoped-for parental approval.

Rugby is a re-enaction of an earlier more primitive bid for power. The struggle in the scrum, the battle to be the first to pick up the ball and run, may reflect an earlier need to break out and make a dash for it. Those who play or watch one form of football or the other seldom intermix. Parental attitudes will have been different. The kickers, by definition, are more violent. Many are likely to have had mainly male siblings with whom they played rough and tumble games. The handlers on the other hand, are essentially non-violent. They embrace. Their girlfriends watch them and share their sweaty pleasures vicariously.

Professional basketball is invariably a male province. The powerful stature and macho image of the players provides them with a strong defence against highly unlikely allegations of effeminacy. They are often in fact accused of being hostile to women because of their notorious 'love them and leave them' attitudes. Once a player gets it in (the net), he turns away and plays with his friends. The basketball player may be attracted to women willing to accept exploitive male penetrative behaviour. In 1991, one time superstar Magic Johnson was reported as having caught AIDS from a call girl. The *New York Times* quoted a number of prominent sports figures who had complained that prostitutes were endangering athletes, but the *Today* newspaper, in a twist that suggested that athletes were endangering prostitutes, claimed that the thirty-two-year-old star was a notorious womaniser who refused to wear condoms. 'He just couldn't get enough,' said one conquest. 'Magic was like a wild man. It's no shock to anyone who knows him that he's got AIDS. He's been playing with fire.' Magic may have been a womaniser, but there were plenty of women used to being exploited at first by abusive mothers and perhaps later by abusive fathers, who allowed themselves to be used by Magic and by others like him.

Tennis attracts those who enjoy placing the ball in someone else's court. Unwilling to accept responsibility for their actions, some derive gratification from playing with each other. The self-reported gay affairs of one-time superstar Martina Navratilova were the tip of the lesbian iceberg and there are said to have been at least a dozen gay post World War Two Wimbledon women's champions. Women tennis players never play with men. They are brought up from an early age to play with one another. If you can't beat her join her may be the attitude of small girls whose mothers overpower them. It may be years before tennis provides them with an opportunity to redress the balance in their favour. Tennis, which illustrates the desire of a woman to gain mastery over another woman, reflects the intense rivalry and hostility of many professional players. When the acquisition of such mastery is not possible, a homosexual relationship may prove almost as rewarding. The urge for power can be insatiable. In 2006, the forty-nine-year-old Navratilova, nine times former Wimbledon champion, made a final (unsuccessful) attempt to win one more Wimbledon title.

In 1993, the average age of the top ten women tennis players was twenty (including Martina Navratilova who was then thirty-six). The game has understandably provided a forum for a duel between 'sisters' (in the case of Venus and Serena Williams they actually are sisters) who slam the ball back and forth at one another at ever increasing speeds. As they compete for their father's love, their ambitious women-hating fathers (who have brought their daughters up to be as men) have been known to scream 'Kill her' from the stands. No longer always a game, same-sex tennis has become a post-oedipal fight to win the love of a father and bring about the defeat of a (potential if not actual) mother. One journalist watching Monica Seles and Jennifer Capriati playing to kill commented: 'That was a tennis match played by axe-murderers.'

Professional male tennis players have come to rely so heavily on power, with the service becoming ever faster and more devastatingly 'penetrative', that other manifestations of sexuality are unnecessary. The world record for the fastest service to date was achieved by Andy Roddick, playing against Lleyton Hewitt in 2004, with a speed of 155 mph. Tim Henman had to be satisfied by the outpourings of 'Henmania' generated by his female fans.

Chess, unlike tennis, relies uniquely on skill and memory for what has been described as a war of attrition. No nursery violence, but an intellectual debate between siblings wishing to get their point across. Although muscular activity is virtually non-existent, stamina and physical fitness are essential. Across the chessboard the ruling passion is hate, rather than love. Masters and Grandmasters compete intellectually, believing that nothing else will bring them the affection they crave. One exception was when Steve McQueen played Faye Dunaway in *The Thomas Crown Affair*. The erotic handling of the chessmen and the glances exchanged by the players provided sexual imagery so intense that it was as if a courtship were taking place. More often it is strategies, such as hypnosis, or blowing smoke into the eyes of an opponent (before smoking was banned) that have been employed in the past. With skill the only weapon at his disposal, the sensitive player, prevented from employing other methods of defence or attack, may experience exaggerated feelings of vulnerability amounting in some cases to paranoia. Gary Kasparov is said to have believed that in his early matches behind the Iron Curtain with Anatoly Karpov, the KGB was conducting a dirty tricks campaign against him. The skill of the chess player, free from the exhibition of violence which is sometimes a feature of other competitive games, encapsulates both power and sexuality. While the winner is 'king', the loser – a less than 'grand' master – is (metaphorically) castrated.

Golf is about powerlessness rather than power. Although women also are keen golfers, until relatively recently they were excluded by some clubs from playing at the same time as men. The sexes were separated not only in the changing rooms but also in the clubhouse. The explanation for this probably lay in the hints of dysfunctional sexuality, or the fear of it, inherent in the game. Golf may sometimes be seen as an alternative sexual activity for those with strong loving needs who – perhaps because 'lovelessness' is what they may have been brought up to expect – have an unsatisfactory sex life. The purpose of the game for the male player is 'to get it up' and 'get it in'. 'Never up, never in', is an apparently pointless comment on the green to a player whose ball has stopped short of the hole. This sexual innuendo may overwhelm the more self-conscious male who will avoid mixed foursomes and play exclusively with same-sex partners. Driving the ball off the tee occasionally makes even the most skilful player feel impotent. When poor tee shots are the rule, rather than the exception, they may indeed be a reflection of sexual impotence. The golfer's repeated failure to sink his putts on the green is known as 'the yips', a form of repetitive strain injury, which is understandably rare in women. The player's fear of 'losing his grip' while putting could also conceal his fear of failing to achieve vaginal penetration. Successful treatment of sexual problems in golfers often results in improvement in their game. It is no coincidence that one particular putter which requires the two balls painted on its upper surface to be lined up with the actual ball before striking it, has done wonders for sexually hesitant males.

The premature ejaculator's problem on the golf course, as elsewhere, is manifest through timing. He may arrive in the clubhouse well before his booked play-off time. He will usually also arrive too early for business and social appointments. On the golf course, as in bed, the premature ejaculator is hasty and uncontrolled. A fast swing is likely to result in a missed ball, but a second attempt (in golf as in sex) will often produce more satisfactory results.

> Donald, an up and coming golf professional, had recently fallen in love for the first time. His attractive and vivacious girlfriend was supportive and encouraging but was inadvertently putting him under pressure. Donald felt her expectations difficult to live up to. Premature ejaculation began to threaten their relationship and indirectly his golf. Successful treatment cured the sex problem and by extension the golf problem.

The delayed or absent ejaculator, by contrast, will spend so long rooted to the spot before taking his shot, that he is also easily recognised. Another manifestation of this reluctance to 'give' is his aversion to buying the drinks after the game.

> Kevin, a thirty-year-old golf professional, came home one afternoon to find his wife in bed with the assistant pro at his club. He became so seriously undermined by this that he left his wife and not only became impotent later with another woman, but lost his standing in world-class golf.

Like other 'hurry up' sports (a refrain heard often by dilatory children), equestrianism (other than polo) is mainly about competition against the clock, and is remarkably dangerous. At least thirty people a year in Britain suffer spinal injuries through riding accidents, resulting in permanent paralysis. Children form an attachment to horses at an early age. From around the time of puberty, small girls in particular fall in love with their horses. A girl's involvement with a symbol of an insufficiently available parent is entirely appropriate. The horse, whatever its gender, is experienced as male with male-related characteristics. It is powerful, upright, thrusting and supportive. It is understandable that a growing girl uses her horse rather than her father, as a foil for her developing sexuality.

Adolescent boys (with hormonal and genetic factors contributing to sexual orientation), who have an absentee father and a smothering mother, are additionally encouraged towards same-sex partnerships. The boy's attachment to his horse is also as to a father. Boys who fall in love with their horses could account for the many homosexuals involved with training and riding. 'Being at one with one's horse' creates a unique partnership in show jumping and dressage, but a 'divorce' (from the horse) usually occurs when post-adolescent cross-gender relationships are sought.

'Dipping one's oar into the water', suggests an intermittent short-lived involvement, the excluding of long-term commitment and a hint of only momentary intimacy. Many of those addicted to rowing are re-enacting the intermittent encounters of a fragmented upbringing. Many will not be aware that they are unable to make long-term relationships until they become too old for the strenuous physical activity essential to their chosen sport. When the oarsman's resentment at having been only intermittently loved by childhood care-givers can no longer be sublimated, he may be destined to act out his anger by scapegoating women. The oar above the hearth can never be a satisfactory substitute for a loving commitment in front of it. The female oarsman (participants are referred to as oarsmen irrespective of gender) has no such problems. Her firm grasp of the oar, underlines her commitment to cross-gender sex.

Rowing is competitive and power driven. It demands the ultimate in fitness, timing, skill and co-ordination. Its range extends from the lonely oarsman, through coxless pairs, to the eights in the Oxford and Cambridge boat race which capture the public imagination.

An elderly, sometime Oxford rowing blue, found difficulty living up to his sexually active wife's expectations of him. His sexual orientation, more in keeping with the 'all for one' male ideal of his former crew, led eventually to the end of his marriage. He accepted his impotence and even the divorce with fortitude, but never forgot his wife's taunt that in the boat race he had collapsed over his (phallic) oar at the finishing line.

Motor racing induces hyperarousal in both competitor and spectator. Identifying with the power of the car evokes feelings of omnipotence. Grand Prix Formula One racing, one of the most prestigious, expensive, remunerative and exciting of all sporting events, exemplifies the sterility of power when it is not linked to creativity. 'Dicing with death', the highest stake of all for the unloved risk-taker, evokes levels of exhilaration which will sometimes produce irreversible changes in heart function and at the least a massive increase in heart rate during the race. What is achieved by this tremendous outburst of energy? Certainly nothing creative, since the outcome is occasionally fatal. James Hunt, a one-time Formula One world champion, survived the vicissitudes of his racing career, to die in his bed from a heart attack.

The omnipotent but often 'broken-hearted' drivers on the Grand Prix circuits know that the most they can hope for is to spend their lives going round and round in circles, getting nowhere fast. The repetitiveness of this pattern appeals to those whose aversion to progress is matched only by an inability to make commitments. A wish for a new sexual partner is present in the mind of the racing driver each time he starts his circular journey. An existing sexual partnership may be wound down as soon as he has seen off the competition and crossed the finishing line.

Team managers are known to claim that they have never known men more promiscuous than racing drivers. They are indubitably potent, but their power is illusory since the sexual consequences of it are swallowed up in the eroticism of the vehicle and the excitement of the journey. There is nonetheless no shortage of 'pit babes' attracted to the potency of the racing car and the men who drive them. The underlying motivation for the racing driver is to complete the circuit faster than his opponents, and by so doing, carry off the prize for which he has risked his life. He does not realise that the racing circuit may well symbolise nothing more than the enclosing arms for which he has continued to search since he was denied this satisfaction as a child.

The racing driver's ongoing power struggle with his siblings begins afresh each time he is on the grid. His aim will be either to demonstrate the fruits of victory – triumphantly uncorking a champagne bottle – or reluctantly to accept an amicable defeat with all passion spent. The risk-taking driver however, will never give up his fight to be a winner. Motor racing remains a gamble that he must eventually lose. The arousal generated by the sport merely provides compensatory but illusory alternative nurturing which he must accept as second prize. If he succeeds in passing the finishing line ahead of the other competitors, the illusion of returning to the encircling arms of the mother may then be re-enacted by starting a new sexual relationship. He may insist upon deviant sex, often with sado-masochistic features, but the relationship, like all his previous ones, will come to an end when his new partner demands a commitment. Should he agree to it, the relationship will have incestuous undertones, and will be swiftly abandoned as sex becomes distasteful. He will have no idea why having found his 'mother' in his partner she becomes sexually unattractive to him. He will return to the track to experience once more another illusory embrace, which will inevitably stand in the way of making a more appropriate adult commitment elsewhere.

Fox hunting (banned in 2005) – man's cruelty to animals – is for some a socially acceptable alternative to man's cruelty to man. Those who followed the hunt did so because it excited a dimly remembered passion over and above that which one would expect to find in non-violent leisure activities. Common rationalisations for cruelty to animals, such as 'if you don't kill the fox they will get at the chickens', barely acknowledges the fact that the chicken's life is in any event doomed, and whether it is killed by man or fox can be of little interest to it. 'It's great fun and the fox hardly ever gets killed', 'deer need culling', 'the hare has a good chance of getting away', and 'the hounds need the exercise', are other frequently heard rationalisations. Those who oppose cruelty to animals, whether for sport or for consumption, identify with the helpless. In touch with the neglected child in themselves, they are always angry with the neglectful in others. In many cases the pros and the antis are as violent as one another.

Violence in sport falls into two categories, personal and vicarious. Fox hunting, deer stalking, hare coursing and bull fighting allow for the killing by the participant of his frightened victim, while cock fighting, bear baiting and dog fighting give the spectator – with no danger to himself – the opportunity to watch animals killing one another. Vicarious cruelty is illegal on the specious grounds that to arrange for animals to kill one another is not sporting (although it would seem to be natural), but personal cruelty (hunting) was not only once sanctioned by society (ironically frequently on a Sunday), but became a fashionable indulgence for the wealthy. Killing for sport may for some be sexually arousing and associated with male power equivalents such as the gun or the horse.

Although small game hunting remains legal, big game hunting does not. This prohibition is not humanitarian but ecological, and based on the need to conserve species that in previous generations were virtually extinguished. Many go on safari to compare the power of animals with their own. From the safety of a four-wheel drive, the tourist intrudes into the privacy of wildlife with his binoculars, or 'shoots' the animals with his camera, its long lens providing the illusion of bravery. This distanced power arouses but is not frightening.

Fishing, generally a male obsession, is cold, wet and boring to some and to others pleasurable and addictive. Is the addict 'fishing' for attention? Or is he recalling his unsatisfactory upbringing with another cold fish? The fishing addict repeatedly dips his rod into the water until he succeeds in catching the fish, only to act out his anger by battering it to death. If the fish is too small and beneath his contempt, he throws it back. Such hostility, in the guise of sport, would be hard to equal.

Mountaineering attracts both men and women. Climbing is the acting out of a paradox. The mountaineer believes that the pinnacle of success will continue to elude him. At the same time he fears that if he does achieve it, he will not be able to cope with it. He has however a strong sense of purpose and is compelled to challenge his fear. In so doing he becomes addicted to the high levels of arousal that result from it. Those determined to conquer heights are more often than not phobic about heights. Phobia and counterphobia (fear and the compulsion to confront the fear) provide the stimulus that leads the phobic climber to continue challenging the hostile mountain. He anticipates that it will reject him as did the (mountain-like) breast of his mother during his infancy. If this had gratified him in the past, he might not be as determined to repeat his need to conquer other peaks in the present.

The greater the downside risk the more arousing it is for the adrenaline addict. The greatest downside risk of all is death. The adrenaline generated by dicing with death provides momentary relief from the depression caused by parenting losses and gives the totally unloved a potential, but respectable, escape from life. When these techniques cease to be available through age or infirmity, depression often results. The 'high' achieved through dangerous sport is little different from the 'high' achieved by those who abuse mind-altering drugs. The risk-taker's aim is to rise above the pain of deprivation and to put an end to suffering. As in anaesthesia during surgery however, a safe return cannot always be guaranteed.

14

The Act of Creation

Art is an activity by means of which one man, having experienced a feeling, intentionally transmits it to others.

Leo Tolstoy

Creativity allows a socially acceptable, non-dangerous and often fulfilling re-enactment of the feelings generated by parental neglect. It provides autobiographical insights into the childhood of the artist and to a lesser extent into the childhood of those who – even for a brief moment – are at one with the artist's feelings. No skills are needed for the appreciation of any form of art at this level. Those on the receiving end may not share the artist's talent but this does not preclude them from participating in his early memories.

> Belinda was a deeply depressed thirty-five-year-old maritime artist. Her childhood with an alcoholic, virtually absentee mother and an unloving father was repeatedly depicted in wintry paintings of sailing boats with their sails torn away by violent winds and about to sink in overwhelming seas. Reviewing the occasions when she almost 'went under' during her cold childhood, Belinda was able to recall other memories which in time helped her to come to terms with and ultimately let go of the sadness of her early life.

The passionate and powerful attack on his material by the sculptor provides him with an outlet for his aggression. If the form he struggles to create is that of a woman might it be that it was his mother whom he saw as being made of stone? The female form may represent his vision of perfection and the fulfilment of his dreams. His aim is likely to be the recreation of the mother he would like to have had but of whom he believes himself to have been deprived.

Michelangelo, who was handed over to a wet nurse when he was about a month old, scarcely knew his biological mother who died when he was six. His portrayals of the Madonna and the Christ child and later of Il Papa (the father) Pope Julius II seem to represent a plea for recognition and approval from unavailable parents. It was in his recreation of himself and the family that had excluded him, that he achieved his greatest potency. Michelangelo never married and his interest in women was confined to cold marble. The beauty of his male nudes suggests that his feelings towards men and boys were, by contrast, warm and intimate. Is his *David* making a silent but eloquent statement (to his mother): 'I am beautiful. Everyone admires me. Why did *you* abandon me?'

Artistic creation, like gestation and birth, arises out of heightened arousal which may be compared with sexual arousal. (Elvis Presley is said to have spontaneously ejaculated on one occasion while performing one of his compositions). The 'baby' that results compensates for what the artist perceives to have been lacking in his relationship with his mother. It is a sad reminder of the absence of fulfilment at the breast, and the comfort which should have been provided by his mother's voice. The talented will strive to fill the resulting vacuum.

Those who listen to music discover a spiritual satisfaction which echoes a distant past. Shakespeare seemed to be aware that music, food and love are interchangeable and that music could also fulfil nutritional and loving needs (*Twelfth Night*). Might music also therefore be a substitute for absent mothering? Were childhood care-givers more freely available such substitutions would not be necessary but music lovers would be left hungry.

Italian Renaissance painters used the canvas to relieve castration anxiety (the loss of the penis which Freud believed the male child feared as the penalty for his unrequited love for his mother). Artists face this fear by representing the penis as another part of the body, such as the hair. Many artists – often homosexual, who have themselves turned away from the vagina – would be far too anxious to depict their fears more transparently. Samson, whose hair represented his power, lost his strength when he allowed the prostitute, Delilah, to discover the source of his potency. Cutting his hair while he was drunk and delivering him to the Philistines who blinded him, caused him not only to be brought 'eyeless to Gaza', but also rendered him impotent. While the loss of eyes according to Freud symbolises the loss of testicles, the loss of hair symbolises the loss of the penis. Rembrandt's post-coital Samson is man at his most impotent, immediately after sexual intercourse.

In many sixteenth- to nineteenth-century paintings, castration is also represented by displacing it from the penis to the head. Mantegna's *Judith and Holofernes* has Judith decapitating Holofernes (rendering him powerless). On the same subject Lucas Cranach shows the head of Holofernes held by the hair by the naked Judith. Having successfully robbed her adversary of his potency, she now flourishes it in the phallic (castrating) sword which she wields in her other hand.

Caravaggio shows the boy David with the head of Goliath, illustrating a young boy's wish to emasculate the powerful father with whom he would as a child have been in competition for his mother's love. In another version, Salomé daughter of Herodias and one of the women present at the crucifixion of Jesus asks for the head of John the Baptist as a reward for her dancing. Although Salomé does not personally kill John the Baptist, the (male) executioner in *The Beheading of John the Baptist* (Bachiacca) suggests the sadistic castration of a male rival.

While these paintings do not specifically depict sexual activity, they do reflect presexual emotions that the artist may as a child have experienced with his mother. Those with disturbed personalities may act out their childhood problems through violent conflict, the artist can re-enact them through his work.

By the middle of the nineteenth century, Degas was using his canvas to express his perception of women. He had probably never forgotten having been abandoned after the death of his mother when he was thirteen. He grew up suspicious of all women and claimed that his reason for remaining single was that a wife might dismiss his work (his babies) as his mother had dismissed him as a child (by dying). His female nudes illustrated this rejection. Although many of his women are engaged in making themselves beautiful they do not appear to be making themselves beautiful for him, since he painted many of them with their backs turned.

Graffiti tend to evoke more of a response in the artist than in the observer. Confused with, and contaminated by, political prejudices, graffiti pander to the exhibitionistic and risk-taking sexual needs of the perpetrator. If there is a message to unloving mothers, it does not make itself clear. An exception is the pavement artist, whose gallery is the street and whose chosen place of work reflects the impermanency of his lifestyle, his lack of finances and possibly his expectations. The street artist Bansky, whose work evolved out of his anti-establishment graffiti, is now recognised by some as an establishment artist, but by others as a vandal. His message has yet to be understood.

Francis Bacon converted his disturbed childhood into art which depicted a lifetime of suffering. 'My work is like a diary. To understand it, you have to see how it mirrors my life.' Picasso's comment applies more obviously to Bacon than to many other artists who have been more successful in concealing their emotions. Bacon's cruel and sadistic father, who resented his son's sensitivity and ill health, drove him to look for fatherly love from the homosexual grooms on his estate. Bacon grew up with few of his nurturing needs satisfied. Gratification such as gambling and alcohol were to become compulsive but illusory alternatives. His paintings reflect the tortured images of his abused childhood, his personal visions, and the absence of a God (the father) who failed to rescue him. His output probably mirrors his identification with other father-forsaken sufferers, just as his 'messy' studio was a reflection of his inner chaos. Although not a violent man, Bacon was a victim of violent childhood abuse. He paints out, rather than writes out, the story of his life. George Dyer, the last of his many lovers – whom Bacon is said to have met when he burgled his house – was, like the stable boys of his childhood, guilty of 'forcible entry'. He might have forced his way into Bacon's home, but was subsequently invited into his life.

The socially unacceptable, and of necessity, repressed feelings of nineteenth-century poets were expressed through symbolism. No one illustrated the attitudes to loss in the Victorian age better than Tennyson who was concerned with moral and spiritual issues. His journey to the Pyrenees as a young man of twenty-one, with his close friend, Arthur Hallam, provided him with the inspiration for *In Memoriam*. In this long poem, a non-violent vehicle for emotions he may never have clearly recognised, he commemorated his friend's death three years later. He was, however, pleased to know that Queen Victoria (who would of course, in keeping with the time, have taken the poem at face value and not considered its homoerotic undertones) had read and enjoyed it. Tennyson's 'universal themes' were 'simple, sensuous and passionate', and he happily rationalised the expression of deeply buried emotions. At the age of forty-one, he married – probably for social rather than sexual reasons – after a ten-year engagement. He remained faithful however both to his poetry and to the memory of his friend.

By the second half of the twentieth century, poetry became more explicit and the poet less afraid to reveal himself. Philip Larkin made an attack on his conditional upbringing in the often-quoted *This Be The Verse*: 'They fuck you up, your mum and dad. They may not mean to, but they do. They fill you with the faults they had. And add some extra, just for you.' Larkin was in his forties before he was able to express feelings about his own childhood which had come 'rather late for him' to make major changes in his life.

Larkin never married (he was engaged for a time in the 1940s to Ruth Bowman), but had numerous friends to whom he wrote many thousands of letters, 700 of which were published posthumously. Larkin loved books and spent his life surrounded by them. His literary output was extensive and for thirty years he was a librarian at Hull University. Such was his anxiety about his literary passion (possibly because of the feelings expressed in it) that he ordered much of his *oeuvre* to be destroyed after his death. He had kept in touch with his parents but mainly by letter and continued to write to his widowed mother for thirty years after the death of his father. The warmth of these communications was understandably qualified by the distanced form they took, a continuing reminder of his detached upbringing which was not only cold and conditional but one at arm's length.

Autobiographical information, which provides insight into the writer and his upbringing, is often encoded in his work. The inarticulate find it easier to confide to the page the need for acknowledgement of their worth by parents who may have been deaf to their needs. The *Song of Solomon,* essentially an instruction manual for married couples, is also an erotic plea for parental love. *Lysistrata* (Aristophanes) links female sexuality to power and control, and *Coriolanus* (Shakespeare) – in which Coriolanus's love for his mortal enemy made him a traitor – suggest that the need to exploit sex as a vehicle to compensate for an unloved childhood has remained constant.

Accounts of homoerotic and heteroerotic love, either disguised or explicit, were the forerunners of the romantic fiction of the late twentieth and early twenty-first century. Writers with a disharmonious childhood are likely to depict sex more as deviant and violent, than as an act of love. They will exploit the needs of the pathologically inquisitive and the sexually impoverished with which they readily identify. Crime novels appeal to those whose parents' unpredictable attitudes continue to puzzle them. Like the crime writer, the reader seeks justice, envies (successful) delinquency and identifies with deception. 'Getting away with it' is gratifying to both reader and writer.

Both classical literature and modern fiction allow the writer's past to speak for itself through metaphor and allusion. Those who make use of the 'stream of consciousness' unload persisting and unresolved traumas in their own lives, revealing sensitive issues which otherwise might have been discussed privately with a psychotherapist. While many writers believe that 'getting it off their chests' will inhibit their creativity, being in touch verbally with aspects of the self through therapy can only be an advantage. The writing, acting and directing skills of Woody Allen were probably enhanced by his twenty-five years in psychoanalysis.

Charles Dickens was ten years old when his father was sentenced to the debtor's prison at Marshalsea, leaving his mother to cope alone with their eight children. This traumatic period in his life was reflected in his novels notably *The Pickwick Papers* and *Little Dorrit* (the debtors' prison) and *David Copperfield* (childhood deprivation). Dickens, who appeared to have suffered from separation anxiety, had a life-long fear of the dark and was afraid of death, the ultimate separation. A frequent visitor to the Paris Morgue, where unclaimed bodies were exhibited to the public for identification, he described being 'dragged by invisible force' (presumably his unhappy childhood) into it. The solitude and darkness of the morgue highlighted, and would have reflected, his childhood anxiety when the parents, upon whom he depended but who were often unavailable, had gone to sleep.

Dickens's childhood was not a happy one. His identification with the impoverished children of Victorian England was a reminder of his own need for loving input from parents too involved with their own poverty to provide it. He was never able to relate to women and felt that they did not understand him. He initiated social change by bringing to the attention of his readers, the plight of exploited, hungry and abused children who, like himself, were unable to speak for themselves.

Through acting, illicit sex and his search for fame, Dickens also turned to some of the compensatory mechanisms of the emotionally deprived, and died knowing that he was wealthy and successful. Through his account of life in Victorian England he may have hoped that future generations would be made aware of his own anxieties and his search for love and acceptance. His writing enabled him to relive the traumas of his childhood, which not only acted as a catharsis for his emotional problems, but also saved him from the financial problems of his impoverished family.

His anxiety (about separation and death) appeared to have been recognised by his family. On his death in 1870, Dickens was laid out in the dining room of his home at Gad's Hill Place near Rochester in Kent, the house in which he had dreamed of living since he first saw it at the age of nine. The curtains were drawn back so that the room was filled with sunlight. His portrait, as a young man, was placed above his coffin which was covered with scarlet geraniums, and which echoed a need, about which he often spoke, for brightness and colour. Immortality had come too late to comfort him although it was ensured by his body of work, his burial place in Westminster Abbey and by Gad's Hill Place's conversion into a school.

Writing in France at about the same time as Charles Dickens in England, Gustave Flaubert describes his heroine Emma Bovary's fruitless search for the love which her upbringing had denied her. Her father was incapacitated by a broken (impotent) limb. Her mother loved her only conditionally. Far from 'resting on her laurels' Emma burns the laurel wreath earned at school and searches elsewhere for the love which her austere upbringing had denied her. She is disappointed with her marriage to the local doctor who had treated her father's fracture (symbolically restoring his potency). Unable to use her parents' marriage as a role model, Emma like her begetter himself (whose upbringing with a smothering and male-like mother and a frequently unavailable doctor father had contributed to his own homoeroticism) seeks compensation in sex for the emotional deficits of her childhood.

DH Lawrence was born in Nottinghamshire at about the same time as Sigmund Freud was publishing the first of his papers on childhood sexuality in Vienna. His father Arthur Lawrence, whom he hated, was an alcoholic miner and his mother, Lydia Lawrence, a former teacher. She and his father were in constant conflict and it was her son to whom his mother looked to as an ally and a source of comfort. Lawrence was twenty-seven when he wrote *Sons and Lovers,* a supposedly fictional, but clearly accurate, account of his childhood. Lydia lived for her son and perhaps also died for him, since Lawrence was said to have assisted her in her final illness in 1910 by giving her an overdose of sleeping pills.

Lawrence's accounts of sexual activity show insights into the problems of adults from emotionally deprived backgrounds. An avid reader himself, he could well have been influenced by Freud's ideas on infantile sexuality. His wife Frieda – who had connections with the psychoanalytic movement – is known to have discussed Freud's work with her husband. He was particularly interested in the Oedipus complex, thought to have influenced *Sons and Lovers.* The late nineteenth- and early twentieth-century world however, was not ready for psychological insights into aberrant behaviour whether from the pen of Freud or of Lawrence. Nonetheless Lawrence expressed feelings which he would have been unable to share with anyone. Freud and Lawrence, although for different reasons, were united in their urge to throw light on family life. Freud's method of treating mental illness, which he believed arose entirely out of the dysfunctional upbringing of those who suffered from it, was to allow himself to be used as a blank screen on to which his patients could project their problems. This necessitated listening to them and interpreting their thoughts to them. Lawrence sought to download his own problems on to the page, a less than helpful witness to the problems with which he had grown up and which caused him so much suffering.

Sons and Lovers echoes aspects of Lawrence's early life. Walter Morel, like Lawrence's father was a miner, and his wife (like Lawrence's mother) was smothering and overwhelming. His portrayal of Morel as a weak and non-authoritarian bully can be read as a slightly milder version of his own father. Lawrence's intensely creative, but relatively short life, was spent in a promiscuous search for sexual passion both in his restless journeying round the world, and in his later literary output. He was jealous of Frieda's two children from her first marriage, and was said to have been unable to respond to her sexually. This could well have been due to his over involvement with her role as 'mother'. Unable to free himself of the incestuous attachment to his own mother, Lawrence had made each subsequent relationship seem like an act of infidelity. His hope that on his mother's death [he] 'would not follow her into the darkness' was not to be realised.

Lawrence found women hard to please and, in *Lady Chatterley's Lover,* reveals his own wish to bring physical feelings and responses back not only into everyday life but into his own life. Some see his probing sexuality as unacceptably phallic (although it would be hard to consider it otherwise). They interpret 'the passional secret places' as belonging to Connie's body, or to the bodies of women in general, rather than to the unexplored areas of social life in England as Lawrence may have intended.

Writers seem able to produce their best work when they remain both identified with, and attached to the mother, the source of their creative energy. In addition to his attachment to his mother, the novelist and playwright Henry James was also attached in fantasy to Paris – the mother of all cities and a life enhancer for exiles from less inspirational areas. In Paris he might have found some psychological compensation for his rumoured absence of sexual potency, which he claimed was caused by injury when he was eighteen. This physical explanation for his absence of heterosexual interest would have been more acceptable at the time than a disclosure of homosexuality. He was unable to emphasise a sexuality that he did not possess, but compensated for it with the potency of his writing.

Unlike Henry James, James Joyce dealt with his reactions to his unsolicited gift by attacking not only his own mother but also Mother Church. He turned away from both although remained in touch with his mother through his writing, and famously through his incontinent prose style which could well have reflected an earlier incontinence with which his mother would have been obliged to deal. His life was spent in search of artistic freedom and licence which was not available to him in Ireland at the time. He was essentially an imaginative, sensitive and musically gifted man, who wanted to study medicine but instead became involved in the arts. Like those of Henry James, Joyce's sexual needs seemed to have been fulfilled through his writing and other than an ongoing liaison with Nora Barnacle – a girl from Galway with whom he lived from 1904, and eventually married in 1931 and by whom he had two children – his actual sexuality appears to have remained suppressed.

Writers and their mothers are generally at one with one another. The victims of parental deprivation need not turn to crime to source their needs. Writers write out their story, painters paint it out, sculptors hammer it out, and actors act it out. Even criminals who fight it out and convert order into chaos can, with forethought, choose instead, as indeed many do, to convert chaos into order.

Afterword

The hopes and aspirations of the donor of the 'gift of life' frequently take precedence over the needs and expectations of the recipient. 'Mummy knows best' is more likely to reassure the mother than the child. But does Mummy always know best?

In *An Unsolicited Gift* I have attempted to demonstrate that often it is the child who knows best. If the mother recognises and fulfils her child's needs, later conflict will be avoided and will be replaced by harmony. From the moment of birth, donor and recipient of the gift must talk to one another in a language which both of them will understand. Most mothers correctly interpret their infants' body language and infants intuitively tune into and understand their mothers' babble talk. This early conversation is vital to avoid, at first, misunderstandings between mother and child, and later, misunderstandings with others.

Not every mother agrees that an infant's needs be immediately satisfied and that he should never be kept waiting. But these are his (human) rights and he depends upon his mother to respect them. Should he be denied these rights he may later fail to respect the human rights of others. When the old world – when he was 'within' his mother – is gradually replaced by a new world, when he is 'without' her, he will gradually learn to fend for himself and interests appropriate to his potential will be developed. The child who has had satisfactory input from his parents will find it easy to make a commitment later in life. He will be contented.

Only the child whose early needs have been ignored and who is angry, will choose a destructive lifestyle or, in some cases, a creative one in which his violent impulses may be sublimated.

In the foregoing chapters I have attempted to show the influence that parents, particularly mothers, have on every aspect of their children's lives. Understanding the power of this influence will help parents to interact more thoughtfully with their children. Small changes in small families will lead to large changes in society. If the

foregoing has thrown light on the spin-offs from parent/child communication it will have achieved its goal.

Select Bibliography

Ackroyd, Peter, *Dickens*, Vintage, 2002

Ackroyd, Peter, *Oliver Twist*, Mandarin, 1991

Archives of Disease in Childhood, 89 (12), BMJ Publishing Group, 2004

Aristophanes, *The Lysistrata*, BC Penguin Classics, 2003

Atkins, John, *Sex in Literature*, Calder and Boyars, 1970

Bacon, Francis, *On Death*, Kessinger Publishing, 2006

Bacon, Francis, *His Life and Violent Times*, Andrew Sinclair-Stevenson, 1993

Balzac, Honore de, *Physiologie du Marriage*, Paris: M. Levy, 1876

Bancroft, J., *Homosexual Orientation*, British Journal of Psychiatry, 1994

Balbert, Peter, *DH Lawrence and the Phallic Imagination*, Macmillan, 1989

Bettelheim, Bruno, *The Uses of Enchantment*, Thames and Hudson, 1976

Blunkett, David and Pollard, Stephen, *On a Clear Day*, Michael O'Mara, 2002

Bristow, Edward J., *Vice and Vigilance: Purity Movements in Britain since 1700*, Gill and Macmillan, 1977

Brown, Judith R., *Back to the Beanstalk*, California: Psychology and Consulting Associates Press, 1979

Bundage, James A., *Law, Sex and Christian Society in Medieval Europe*, University of Chicago Press, 1987

Burke, Richard E., *The Senator: My Ten Years with Ted Kennedy*, Mass Market Paperback, 1993

Cabezon, Jose Ignacio (Ed.), *Buddhism, Sexuality and Gender*, New York: SUNY, 1992

Carter, Angela, *Sleeping Beauty and Other Favourite Fairy Tales*, London: Victor Gollancz, 1982

Cole, William Graham, *Sex in Christianity and Psychoanalysis*, London: George Allen and Unwin, 1956

Cole, William Graham, *Sex and Love in the Bible*, London: Hodder and Stoughton, 1960

Cole, Martin and Dryden, Windy, *Sex Therapy in Britain*, Milton Keynes – Philadelphia: Open University Press, 1988

Cook, Elizabeth, *The Ordinary and the Fabulous*, CUP, 1969

Cross, Richard, *The Jack Tales*, Boston Mass: Houghton Miflin Company, 1943

Clodd, Edward, *Tom Tit Tot: An Essay on Savage Philosophy in Folk Tale*, London: Duckworth, 1898

Davenport-Hines Richard, *Sex Death and Punishment*, London: Collins, 1990

Flaubert, Gustave, *Madame Bovary*, Random House, 1957

Friedman, Rosemary, 'The Ideal Jewish Woman and Contemporary Society' in *Confrontations with Judaism*, Edited by Philip Longworth, London: Anthony Blond, 1967

Friedman, Dennis, *Inheritance. A Psychological History of the Royal Family*, London: Sidgwick and Jackson, 1993

Froude, Henry, *Poems of Tennyson*, OUP, 1910

Guppy, Shusha, *Looking Back*, Simon and Schuster, 1993

Goldscheider, Ludwig, *Michaelangelo*, Phaidon Press, 1953

Heymann, C. David, *A Woman named Jackie*, 1993

Iona and Peter, *The Classic Fairy Tales*, OUP, 1974

James, Henry, *The Ambassadors*, Wordsworth Classics, 1992

Jeffrey-Poulter, S., *Peers, Queers and Commoners*, Routledge, 1992

Joyce, James, *Ulysses*, The Bodley Head, 1960

Joyce, James, *Dubliners*, Paladin, 1988

Larkin, Philip, *Collected Poems*, Marvell Press, 1988

Langdon-Davis, John, *Sex, Sin and Sanctity*, Gollancz, 1954

Lawrence, DH, *Sons and Lovers*, Penguin Books, 1989

Lawrence, DH, *Lady Chatterley's Lover*, Penguin Books, 2006

Le Saux, G., *Left Field*, HarperSport, 2008

Lexmond, J. and Reeves, R., *Building Character*, London: Demos, 2009

Lucie-Smith, E., *Sexuality in Western Art*, Thames and Hudson, 1991

Miles, Rosalind, *The Children We Deserve*, HarperCollins, 1994

Miller, Alice, *For Your Own Good*, New York: Farrar Strauss Giroux, 1984

McCann, Richard, *Just a Boy*, Ebury Press, 2004

Reade, Brian (Ed.), *Sexual Heretics*, Routledge and Kegan Paul, 1970

Rosen, I., *The Pathology and Treatment of Sexual Deviation*, OUP, 1964

Reik, Theodor, *Of Love and Lust*, Farrar, Strauss and Co., 1941

Spong, John Shelby, *Living in Sin?*, Harper and Row, 1988

Sartre, Jean-Paul, *Anti-Semite and Jew*, New York: Schocken Books, 1948

Shelby, John, *Born of a Woman. A Bishop Rethinks the Birth of Jesus*, San Francisco: Harper, 1992

Schreber, DCM, 'The Harmful Body Positions and Habits of Children', in *Soul Murder: Persecution in the Family* by M. Schetzman, Penguin Books, 1976

Stein, Martha L., *Prostitution in Handbook of Sexology*, Ed. Money and Musaph Excerpta Medica, 1977

Stone, Albert E. Jnr (Ed.), *Twentieth Century Interpretations of The Ambassadors*, NJ: Prentice Hall Inc., 1969

Thwaite, Anthony (Ed.), *Selected Letters of Philip Larkin*, Faber and Faber, 1992

Tolstoy, Leo, *What is Art*, Geoffrey Cumberlege, OUP, 1930

Wilson, Glenn and Rahman Qazi, *Born Gay*, London: Peter Owen, 2006

Zhisui Li, *The Private Life Of Chairman Mao*, Arrow Books, 1996